Tea Cocktails

Tea Cocktails

UNIQUE AND DELICIOUS TEA-INFUSED COCKTAILS

ABIGAIL R. GEHRING *WITH* TEATULIA ORGANIC TEAS

Skyhorse Publishing

Skyhorse Publishing books may be purchased in bulk at special discounts for sales promotion, corporate gifts, fund-raising, or educational purposes. Special editions can also be created to specifications. For details, contact the Special Sales Department, Skyhorse Publishing, 307 West 36th Street, 11th Floor, New York, NY 10018 or info@skyhorsepublishing.com.

Skyhorse® and Skyhorse Publishing® are registered trademarks of Skyhorse Publishing, Inc.®, a Delaware corporation.

Visit our website at www.skyhorsepublishing.com.

10 9 8 7 6 5 4 3 2

Library of Congress Cataloging-in-Publication Data is available on file.

Cover design and photo by Abigail R. Gehring

Print ISBN: 978-1-5107-3796-9
Ebook ISBN: 978-1-63220-760-9

Printed in China

Tea Cocktails

CONTENTS

Forewoid

Welcome to the wonderful world of tea cocktails!

At Teatulia, we are bringing best-quality organic teas to the world for enjoyment in the traditional (hot) fashion. But we are also seeking to make tea "relevant" for all elements of our society at all times of day.

Tea is tremendously versatile, contributes to a healthy lifestyle, and has flavor elements that allow it to pair beautifully with food and spirits. So we figured a book of cocktails would inspire everyone from mixologists to tea experts to neighborhood bbq aficionados to steep some tea, experiment, and enjoy!

We hope you love this book and that it gives you a greater appreciation and affection for the beautiful, timeless *Camellia sinensis* and all of its herbal friends.

Cheers!

Linda Appel Lipsius
CEO and Co-Founder of Teatulia Organic Teas

Introduction

In classy bars and cocktail lounges across America, tea is making a big splash. The only real surprise here is that using tea in cocktails didn't catch on much sooner! Why didn't more people say, "Hey, we should try putting some tea in that Long Island iced tea!"? With such a range of flavors—from sweet and spicy chai to dark and smoky yerba mate—tea is an ideal mixer. It offers nuanced complexity to your cocktails that you simply can't achieve from most traditional cocktail mixers, especially commercially-produced syrups that tend to have overpowering artificial flavor. My first sip of a tea cocktail was, quite honestly, startling—I had thought it might just taste like a watered down mojito, when instead it was brilliantly refreshing, vibrant, and layered with subtle but luscious flavors.

The recipes in this book focus on using healthful ingredients such as fresh fruit juice, herbs, and natural sweeteners, both to give you the best possible flavor and to complement the health benefits of the tea. Enjoyed in moderation, tea cocktails can give your body a boost!

Teatulia Organic Teas is passionate about more than just tea—they care deeply about sustainable gardening practices and social responsibility. Started in 2000 to give back to the community in Bangladesh, they sought an enterprise that would give the Bangladeshi people a living wage while protecting/strengthening the environment. Not content with the social programs already in place in their community, Teatulia's cooperative, the KS Foundation, has established revolutionary education, health, and cattle-lending programs for the people working in the garden and surrounding areas. All sales of Teatulia Organic Teas

contribute to this mission, helping to better the lives of Bangladeshi men, women, and children while rebuilding the local ecosystem. It is an honor to work with such a forward-thinking company on this book.

So put a pot on to boil and call up a friend—it's time for a grown-up tea party!

—Abigail R. Gehring

Tea 101

Tea is one of the oldest herbal remedies in existence, dating back more than 4,700 years when infusions of the plant *Camellia sinensis* were first brewed in China. Although modern medicine has overshadowed many of the ancient cure-alls of our ancestors, the benefits of tea still remain relevant today.

FIRST THINGS FIRST: DEFINING TEA

It's important to understand exactly what qualifies a beverage as "tea." Officially, "tea" refers to black tea, green tea, white tea, oolong tea, or pu-erh tea. The common link between these five categories is that they are each made from the leaves of the *Camellia sinensis* plant. Herbal "teas" aren't actually scientifically considered teas at all because they do not come from the *Camellia sinensis* plant, though they may be commonly referred to as such. These kinds of teas or infusions include chamomile or peppermint, which are made using a variety of different plants with varying nutritional values.

THE FABULOUS FIVE

What makes the five types of teas distinct from one another? The preparation and maturity of tea leaves determine both the flavor and the nutritional content of each type. The leaves used to make black tea are both wilted and fully oxidized, meaning that they are dried and modified through prolonged exposure to air. Green tea goes through the wilting process but not oxidization, while oolong tea leaves are wilted and oxidized but not to the prolonged extent of black tea leaves. White tea is the young tea bud and is neither wilted nor oxidized. Finally, pu-erh tea leaves are fermented.

How is Tea Made?

Teatulia grows and processes all of their teas at their own USDA-certified organic tea garden in Northern Bangladesh's Tetulia region. But how do their fresh, organic tea leaves get from their garden into your teacup (or cocktail glass)?

TYPES OF TEA PROCESSING

There are two basic methods of tea production: Orthodox and non-orthodox. Each method produces a very different final tea product.

ORTHODOX

Process Flow: whole leaf rolled & shaped complex flavor artisan method

The orthodox method uses a process that preserves the integrity and flavor of the tea leaf throughout all stages of production. Whole tea leaves are carefully rolled or shaped into various sizes and styles depending on the type of tea being produced.

An artisan orthodox tea producer can greatly vary the outcome of a tea's final appearance, aroma, and flavor by how the tea leaf is shaped, oxidized, and dried during this process. The orthodox method takes longer, but results in an attractive full leaf tea with complex flavor and aroma.

NON-ORTHODOX

Process Flow: shredded leaf made for tea bags one-dimensional flavor machine method

Also known as Cut-Tear-Curl, or CTC, non-orthodox processing is machine driven and yields small, intentionally shredded pieces of the tea leaf that are shaped into granular pellets. CTC was originally designed for the production of a strong, full-bodied black tea that could be packaged in traditional tea bags and stand up to the added milk and sugar in a brewed cup. This method was created to eliminate some of the labor-intensive steps of the orthodox method in order to speed up time to market for black tea production.

What the CTC process lacks is the ability to produce a wide range of teas and tea flavors. Some green teas can be produced through this method, but white and oolong teas cannot. CTC is mainly a black tea production process because as the leaves are shredded, oxidation starts quickly. CTC-processed leaves are highly oxidized and they start losing their essential oils immediately. Therefore, subtle nuances in aroma and flavor cannot be controlled, creating a final tea product with a one-dimensional profile.

TEATULIA'S ORTHODOX PROCESSING

Teatulia practices the orthodox method of tea production in order to preserve the whole tea leaf, control the outcome of the aroma and flavor of the final tea, and have the ability to produce a variety of tea styles from white to green to black.

Teatulia follows these key orthodox processing steps:

- **Plucking:** Teatulia's tea leaves are hand plucked by the local Bangladeshi men and women who cultivate their tea garden. While the tea bushes are very mature, they are kept pruned to waist-high height so that tea pluckers can easily access the leaves and buds from the youngest, newest growth near the top of the plant.
- **Weighing:** During a typical eight-hour workday in the tea garden, a tea plucker will fill several baskets with fresh tea leaves. When

a basket is full, pluckers take the tea leaves to be inspected and weighed to make sure only the highest quality, undamaged tea leaves are chosen to be processed. On average, 22 to 25 kilograms of processed tea is manufactured from every 100 kilograms of fresh tea leaves.[1]

- **Transporting:** Newly plucked tea leaves are transported directly from their tea garden to their on-site production facility, where the inspecting, sorting, and processing of the leaves into white, green, or black tea begins immediately.

- **Withering:** Freshly plucked tea leaves are fragile and can easily break apart. So as a first step in processing, the leaves are laid out to dry for several hours so they will "wither" and lose some of their moisture content. Withering softens the tea leaves, making them flexible and supple so they won't crumble during the rest of the processing steps.

- **Rolling:** This is where Teatulia tea leaves start developing their unique appearance and flavor profiles. As the soft leaves are rolled and shaped by machine, the cell walls of the leaf are broken, releasing the enzymes and essential oils that will alter the flavor of the leaf. Rolling exposes the chemical components of the tea leaves to oxygen and initiates the oxidation process.

- **Oxidizing:** Oxidation is a chemical reaction that alters the flavor of tea and helps the processed tea develop its ultimate appearance and color. How long the tea leaves are allowed to oxidize, or be exposed to oxygen, will determine the type of tea the leaf will become. Black tea leaves are highly oxidized, and are therefore the darkest in color and strongest in flavor. Oolong teas vary in levels of oxidation and therefore have varying colors and flavors depending on the goals of the tea producer. Green and white teas are light in color and flavor because they are essentially non-oxidized.

- **Firing:** Firing initiates the final drying process. Once the leaf is oxidized to its desired level, heat is applied to the tea leaf to halt the oxidation process and further reduce the leaf's moisture content so that the tea leaves can be stored without spoiling. Depending on the type of heat applied, firing can also lend some flavor characteristics to the final tea.

- **Sorting:** Once the tea leaves have dried, they are visually sorted into various groups of similar size and color to create different lots of like teas. These lots of tea receive different industry grades that rate how the tea visually looks depending on how much whole leaf, broken leaf, or unopened tea buds end up in the lot. These grading systems don't necessarily determine quality, though. The best measure of quality is how the final tea tastes.

- **Tasting:** Before any Teatulia tea travels from our organic garden to make its way into your teacup, they carefully taste every lot to make sure it's of consistently fresh and pure quality. Professional tasters inspect the appearance, aroma, and flavor of the dry tea leaf, infused tea leaf, and brewed tea liquor to make sure what you end up buying and brewing is the finest, freshest tea available.

HOW DO YOU GET WHITE, GREEN, AND BLACK TEAS FROM THE SAME LEAF?

From withering to drying, the same *Camellia sinensis* tea leaf is treated differently during processing to produce the very different aroma and flavor effects of white, green, and black teas.

White: Withering >> Drying. Teatulia's white tea is neither rolled nor fired, so it is essentially non-oxidized and it is the least processed. Instead of being exposed to an artificial heat, the leaves are simply allowed to wither and dry in a carefully controlled environment, which results in the most delicate, fresh-from-the-garden tasting tea.

Green: Steaming >> Rolling >> Firing. Teatulia's green tea is passed through a steaming treatment before rolling. Steaming applies light heat to the leaves to help halt the oxidation process before the leaves are rolled into shape. Steaming also helps expose the fresh, grassy flavor of the leaf. Green tea leaves are not allowed to oxidize after rolling, which is why they remain light in color and flavor.

Black: Withering >> Rolling >> Oxidation >> Firing. The black tea is rolled immediately after withering to help get the oxidation processes started quickly. The leaves are then fully oxidized before they are dried, which is how they get their dark color and rich flavor.

How to Brew Tea

How a tea is brewed can make all the difference between an amazing tea experience and an unremarkable one. So here's Teatulia's primer on all the things to consider when you sit down to brew your next cup of tea.

KNOW YOUR H₂O

Brewed tea is 99 percent water, so the water you start with has a lot to do with the final taste of the brewed tea. If your water tastes "off" or has impurities, then your tea will taste the same, no matter how strong you make your brew. Just remember that it's always best to start your tea experience with fresh, clean water. Filtered or bottled spring water is best; avoid using unfiltered tap, distilled, or mineral water.

12

CONSIDER THE THREE Ts

Before you simply pour hot water over your tea, consider the type of tea you're brewing. Different **types** of tea have different ideal brewing **temperatures** and steeping **times** that will yield the best flavor out of that specific tea. So take a minute to think about the three Ts before you brew:

- **Type:** What type of tea are you planning to brew? Green tea leaves, for example, are more delicate and fresh than black tea leaves, so they can be steeped at a lower temperature and don't need to be steeped as long. Herbal infusions, on the other hand, do not contain the *Camellia sinensis* tea plant, so they can steep much longer than a true tea without becoming astringent or bitter.
- **Temperature:** Tea generally requires a brewing temperature of anywhere from 160 to 212 degrees Fahrenheit, depending on the type of tea. If you don't have an electric kettle with a temperature control, just remember that at sea level water simmers at 190

degrees and boils at 212 degrees. You can visually guesstimate the water temperature by paying attention to the bubbles. But remember that the boiling temperature drops about a degree for every 100 feet in altitude increase, so you may need to adjust depending on how far above sea level you are situated.

- **Time:** If you steep tea for too little time, your tea can be weak and watery. If you over steep your tea, you could risk a mouthful of bitterness and astringency. Taste your tea after the minimum recommended steeping time and then decide if you'd like it to steep a little longer. For cocktails or iced teas, use more tea leaves rather than longer steeping times to make a stronger brew (see page 18).

Here's a little cheat sheet to help you remember the three Ts for the different types of tea you may be brewing:

Tea Type	Temperature	Time
White	160 to 190 degrees F	2 to 5 minutes
Green	160 to 180 degrees F	1 to 3 minutes
Oolong	100 to 200 degrees F	3 minutes
Pu-erh	200 to 212 degrees F	2 minutes
Black	200 to 212 degrees F	3 to 5 minutes
Herbal	200 to 212 degrees F	5 to 7 minutes

Remember that these are general brewing guidelines. The best bet for the perfect tea experience is to start by asking your tea vendor for brewing instructions specific to the tea you purchased. Different teas, even if they come from the same type category (green, black, etc.), can have different ideal brewing temperatures and steeping times.

TEATULIA'S THREE Ts

When you examine your collection of Teatulia teas, you'll notice specific brewing recommendations listed on the packaging for each variety of tea. Below are some general brewing guidelines for the different types of tea, with a visual guideline of what to look for rather than a specific water temperature. Teatulia's teas taste great using these steeping guidelines and you won't have to worry about reaching an exact temperature for each tea.

Teatulia Tea Type	Temperature	Time
Teatulia White Teas	Water just off the boil	3 minutes
Teatulia Green Teas	Water just off the boil	3 minutes
Teatulia Oolong Tea	Boiling water	3 minutes
Teatulia Black Teas	Boiling water	3 minutes
Teatulia Herbal Teas	Boiling water	5 minutes (Ginger: 1 minute)

BOILING POINTS

So you've picked the type of tea you're going to brew and you know your temperature and steeping time goals. Now what? There are so many ways to bring that fresh, clean water to a boil. Here are some of the most popular:

Electric tea kettle: The beauty of this countertop accessory is that it doesn't require a stove and it automatically shuts off when the water comes to a boil, which is typically very quickly. Some electric kettles have built-in temperature control settings so you can select the exact temperature you're trying to reach based on the tea you're steeping.

Stovetop tea kettle: This classic tea kettle sits atop a stove burner to boil and typically has a whistle to alert you when the water has come to a full boil.

Stovetop saucepan: No kettle? No problem. Simply bringing water to a boil in a saucepan on the stovetop is a perfectly acceptable way to prepare hot water for your cup of tea.

Microwave: While this is a quick way to heat water, it leaves a lot to be desired. A microwave does not heat water evenly and different microwaves have different heat levels, so there is no consistent setting to boil water. Even though bubbles might be showing after a minute or so, it doesn't mean the water came to a thorough boil. And since there is no way to gauge boiling point in a microwave, it's also easy to overheat water. Overheated water (above boiling point) loses a lot of oxygen, which can accentuate the impurities in the taste of the water. It can also scorch the tea leaves you're steeping, leaving an excessively bitter brew.

UNDERSTANDING TEA PACKAGING

While your fresh water is coming to a boil, start measuring out your tea. How many cups of tea are you making? Are you starting with loose tea leaves that require a brewing tool? Or did your tea come packaged in some sort of tea bag? Teatulia's teas come in both formats and there are advantages to each.

Loose leaf: Loose leaf tea is tea how it was meant to be. Loose, whole, or partially broken tea leaves are allowed to expand and unfurl as they interact with hot water in a steeping vessel that gives them plenty of room to do so, like a teapot or a roomy strainer that sits in a teacup. The result is a brewed tea that yields all of the subtle flavor nuances its grower and producer intended. A single serving of loose leaf tea is typically measured out as 2 grams of loose tea (about the size of a teaspoon) per 8 ounces of hot water (about the size of a typical tea mug). To brew several cups of tea in a large teapot, simply

increase the amount of loose leaf tea to match the total ounces of water you're using. Loose leaf tea can typically be steeped multiple times, so you can get several brewed cups out of the same measurement of tea.

Pyramid tea bag: Pyramid tea bags were designed to bring the loose leaf tea experience to the convenience of a tea bag. They are tall, roomy bags that fit in a single teacup and give tea leaves plenty of space to move around and fully expand for full flavor extraction. They can also be steeped multiple times, so you can get several cups of tea out of one pyramid tea bag.

Round tea bag: For the ultimate in convenience plus the strong flavor of a full-bodied tea, round paper tea bags are filled with fine-cut tea leaves. The bags fit the shape of your teacup so the water can easily flow through the bag and infuse the tea, resulting in a brew that is fuller-bodied and typically stronger than a pyramid tea bag brew. Each round tea bag is typically steeped just one time.

SELECTING A STEEPING VESSEL

Depending on the type of tea you're brewing, how it was packaged, and how many people you're brewing for, you may choose one of many steeping vessels to create the perfect cup of tea. Here are some of Teatulia's favorites:

Teacup: You can easily steep your favorite tea bag or loose leaf tea in a teacup. For loose leaf tea, you just need a leaf-containing device, like a stainless steel or bamboo brewing basket, or a paper or cloth tea filter. These tools easily sit in your teacup and hold the loose tea leaves. You simply pour the heated water over the contained tea leaves and then remove the device once the proper steeping time is up.

Teapot: Teapots come in almost as many varieties as tea. Teapots that come with a built-in, removable tea strainer or brewing basket to hold loose leaf tea leaves are handy. They allow you to remove the tea leaves from the pot of water after the appropriate steeping time so the tea doesn't over steep. Be sure and adjust the amount of tea you brew to the size teapot you're using. Some pots hold just a couple of cups of tea, while others are designed to brew many cups for a crowd. You can also throw several tea bags into a teapot to achieve a multi-cup brew with easy clean up.

French press: A nice alternative to the traditional teapot, the French press makes a quick and easy tea brewing tool with very easy clean up. Simply add tea leaves or tea bags to the French press, pour in the hot water, and cover with the lid (with filter and screen attached). Allow it to steep for the appropriate amount of time and watch the leaves unfurl, called "the agony of the leaves," then press the tea to the bottom, just like you would coffee grounds. When using a French press, only brew the amount you plan on sipping right away. The tea you press to the bottom of the container will continue to steep in whatever water remains, which could cause some over steeping and make your remaining tea bitter. It's also ideal to use a separate French press for tea and coffee. The flavor of coffee can linger in a French press (no matter how many times you clean it) and it can cause your tea to taste like coffee.

Coffee maker: You can brew your tea in a countertop coffee maker in much the same way you brew your coffee. Simply add loose leaf or tea bag tea to the coffee filter instead of coffee grounds. Then add water to the reservoir, place the carafe on the warmer, and wait for the tea to brew. This is a great option for brewing a large amount of tea for a crowd or if you're planning to make iced tea. Just as with a French press, however, be aware that some coffee flavor can leach into your brewed tea if your coffee maker is mainly used to brew coffee.

Tip: Whichever vessel you're using to steep your tea, remember to always cover your tea while it steeps to help keep as much heat as possible inside the steeping vessel.

TEA ON ICE IS NICE

It's easy to brew an iced tea; it just requires a little forethought. Here are a few of the ways you can enjoy your favorite Teatulia tea on ice:

Straight-up brewing: Brew a cup or pot of hot tea just as you normally would, let it cool down, put it in the refrigerator to chill, and then pour it over ice when you're ready to serve. (If you pour it over ice while it's still hot, the tea will become diluted with melted ice.)

Making a concentrate: In this scenario, you would make a stronger brew by using a higher ratio of tea to water than you normally would for a cup of hot tea. Tea concentrates are ideal for use in cocktails. To make a large batch of iced tea concentrate with your favorite Teatulia tea, steep 15 Teatulia pyramid tea bags in a gallon of boiled water for the recommended amount of time. Then dilute the concentrate when you're ready to sip by pouring it over a glass of ice if it's still hot, or topping it off with fresh, cold water and a little ice if you've let the concentrate chill. If you're only making a small batch, use 1 tea bag per 1 cup of water.

How to Store Tea

A BRIEF HISTORY

It's claimed that tea most likely originated as a medicinal drink in Yunnan, China, during the Shang Dynasty of 1500 BC – 1046 BC. But one popular tea legend suggests that Shennong, Emperor of China and supposed inventor of Chinese medicine, discovered tea as a beverage around 2737 BC when fresh tea leaves from a nearby tea tree fell into his cup of just boiled water. He thought the beverage to be restorative and encouraged its cultivation as a new, medicinal beverage for his people.

In either origin of tea story, it's true that as the popularity of the tea beverage grew, not everyone had access to fresh tea leaves to brew, nor would fresh-picked tea leaves stay fresh very long.

Originally, fresh tea leaves were steamed and compressed into cakes or bricks to dry for easy preservation. The dried tea bricks would then be ground as needed and added to hot water to make a beverage.

The production, preparation, and uses of tea throughout China's history were known to change over time however, based on the whim and directive of the most current emperor and his dynasty of the time.

Eventually, tea masters developed various modern tea production methods—like rolling, oxidizing, and firing—to make distribution and export more manageable, and to ensure tea was treated in a way that it could be shipped and stored by both merchants and consumers without fear of spoiling.

TEA STORAGE TIPS

While the tea produced today won't ever really go bad, it can get stale and lose its flavor. The longer tea sits in your cupboard, the faster it will lose its freshness and originally intended flavor profile, so it's best enjoyed within a few months to a year of purchase.

Here are some general guidelines for storing tea so it remains as fresh as possible for as long as possible:

Know your tea: Buy tea from a reputable company that can tell you when and how the tea was processed and packaged.

Buy small: Buy fresh tea in small quantities and refill when you get low. And date your tea when you buy it, so you know how long it's been on your shelf.

Protect tea from its enemies: Store tea in a cool, dark place away from light, heat, and moisture. Light and heat can activate enzymes that will start to degrade your tea. And tea is shelf-stable because it's completely dry. Any interaction with moisture can drastically shorten the shelf life of tea, so refrigeration or freezing is not recommended.

Don't let tea breathe: The more tea is exposed to oxygen, the higher the chance it will absorb odor and moisture from the air around it. Therefore, it's best to store tea in an airtight, non-plastic, opaque container. Glass, tin, or aluminum containers are best. Plastic can transfer odors and chemicals into the tea and affect the tea's flavor.

Put tea in seclusion: Tea is highly absorbent, so give tea its own storage area far away from coffee, spices, or anything else in your pantry that has a strong odor. If you have flavored teas, store them separately from your non-flavored as flavored teas can impart their flavor into other teas.

The shelf life for tea varies depending on the type of tea, how it was produced, and how you take care of it once you get it home. Here are a few rules of thumb for how long different types of tea can be stored:

Green, white, and herbal teas: These are all delicate teas and infusions that require more careful storage attention and will remain fresh up to a year if cared for properly.

Flavored teas: Teas treated with flavorings, like an Earl Grey flavored with bergamot oil, will have a shorter shelf life of around six months to a year.

Oxidized teas: Darker teas, like oolong and black, that have been exposed to more oxygen in the production process are less sensitive to environmental factors and can last for upwards of two years if stored properly.

   Pu-erh tea: This tea is the exception to the rule. Pu-erh is its own category of tea in which the tea leaves are allowed to age and undergo a natural fermentation process. So like wine, the flavor of pu-erh develops and changes over time. And also like a fine wine, the longer a pu-erh ages, the better its flavor becomes. So most pu-erh tea can be stored (properly) indefinitely.

Tips for Perfect Tea Cocktails

Tea pairs beautifully with a wide range of herbs, fruit juices, and spirits. When crafting a tea cocktail, you want to use ingredients that will complement the tea without overpowering its own unique flavor. Whether you're using the recipes in this book or creating your own signature tea cocktail, here are a few tips.

CHOOSE THE RIGHT INGREDIENTS (BESIDES THE TEA)

SPIRITS

Using high quality spirits will make a noticeable difference in your cocktails—they'll taste and feel more lively and sophisticated. If you don't already have a fully stocked bar, you may want to just purchase the essentials, choosing quality over quantity. The most frequently used spirits are:

- Gin
- Tequila
- Vodka
- Dark or Spiced Rum
- Light Rum
- Bourbon
- Brandy
- Rye Whiskey
- Scotch

If you're new to buying spirits, ask someone at your local liquor store to help you choose bottles that are the highest quality that fit your budget.

FRUITS, VEGETABLES, AND HERBS

Beyond using quality tea leaves, choose fruits and vegetables that are as fresh and ripe as possible. If you're skeptical of the locavore movement, you probably haven't tasted fruits and vegetables that have just been picked. They're like completely different foods than the produce that's been shipped thousands of miles to your supermarket shelves, and they'll take your cocktails to a whole new level of refreshing deliciousness. That said, we don't all have our own gardens. And sometimes even buying local produce isn't practical. But if possible, choose organic. Even if you wash your fruits and vegetables thoroughly, they will have absorbed some of the pesticides and herbicides used on the fields they were grown in, and for all kinds of reasons you don't want to put that stuff in your body. Also, produce that is not grown organically will often contain smaller amounts of the vitamins and minerals your body needs. Now, health may not be the primary goal of enjoying a cocktail, but why not sneak in some extra nutrition when you can?

Frozen produce is also an acceptable alternative in many cases—produce frozen at its peak of ripeness maintains most of its nutrients. Frozen berries work beautifully in frozen, blended cocktails or can be dropped whole into any cocktail instead of ice cubes.

Fruit juice will always taste best when it's freshly squeezed, but if you use bottled juices be sure to choose varieties without added sugar.

SWEETENERS

If using granulated sugar, look for pure cane sugar. If sugar isn't labeled as cane, it is probably made at least partially from beets—and in America, sugar beets are mostly genetically modified. Many of the recipes in this book call for simple syrup made from natural sweeteners, which lend a more complex flavor to the cocktails and have some nutritional benefits.

Honey: The best honey—both for nutrition and flavor—is in its raw form. Raw honey is a powerful antioxidant and has antiviral, antibacterial, and antifungal properties. It strengthens the immune system and can fight allergies (particularly if the honey is from local bees). Honey complements tea perfectly. To make honey simple syrup, see the recipe on page 124.

Maple Syrup: Maple syrup is, well, delicious. I'm from Vermont, so I grew up tapping trees and boiling down the sap to make our liquid gold. Maple syrup doesn't rank quite as high as honey on the health scorecard, but it does have a lot of anti-inflammatory and antioxidant properties. Be sure to use 100 percent real maple syrup, not a syrup that's artificially flavored. Maple syrup can be used directly in your cocktails or made into a simple syrup (see page 128).

Coconut Sugar: Evaporated sap from coconut palm trees, coconut sugar has a delicate caramel flavor similar to brown sugar. It contains many vitamins and minerals and less fructose than cane sugar. To make coconut simple syrup, see page 129.

What about Agave? Agave, sometimes called "the great Mexican aloe," produces a sweet sap, or nectar, that is traditionally extracted from the leaves, filtered, and heated to become a concentrated syrup—sort of like the tropical version of maple syrup. (However, most agave sweeteners you can find in stores come from the blue agave plant, and rather than the sap being extracted from the leaves, it comes from the starchy root bulb. The agave glucose is converted to syrup through an enzymatic and chemical process that is similar to how cornstarch is converted to high fructose corn syrup and results in a product that's very high in fructose. Fructose in highly concentrated forms wreaks havoc on your liver and can result in long-term health problems.)

CHOOSE THE RIGHT TOOLS

You really don't need very many tools for making cocktails, but there are a few things that will help.

- **Ice Cube Trays** for making tea ice cubes (see page 29)
- **Cocktail Shaker**
- **Jigger or Shot Glass** to measure liquids. Most are 1½ ounces. You can also use a clear measuring cup that has liquid ounces marked on it. If you don't have any of these, you can use a regular measuring cup as long as you know that 2 ounces equal ¼ cup.
- **Muddlers** are helpful for gently mashing fruits or herbs in your cocktails, but you can also use the back of a spoon or a pestle.
- **Glasses**: Glass suggestions are included with every recipe in this book but you can use whatever you like. Serve your cocktails in teacups or mason jars if you feel like it!

COCKTAIL GLASSES

Here are the glasses most often referenced in this book, but feel free to use whatever glasses suit your fancy!

Pilsner

Cosmopolitan

Whiskey Sour

Mug

Collins

Martini

Highball

Champagne Flute

Hurricane

Old Fashioned

Margarita

Punch Glass

plan ahead

Tea cocktails will be quickest to mix and taste best if you plan at least a few hours ahead. Brew more tea than you'll need for the cocktails and pour some into ice cube trays to freeze. That way the ice in your drink will add more flavor to your cocktails rather than watering them down. The tea that you don't freeze can be stored in the refrigerator for up to a few days.

Mason jars are perfect for chilling tea until you're ready to prepare your cocktails. If storing several types of tea, be sure to label them.

RECIPES

Light and Fruity Cocktails

Peach Smash with Fresh Mint and White Tea

Glass type: collins or old fashioned

Makes 2 cocktails

TRADITIONAL ENGLISH TEA IS SERVED MIDAFTERNOON AND IS ACCOMPANIED WITH SCONES AND CLOTTED CREAM OR OTHER SWEETS OR TEA SANDWICHES—THE LATER IT IS SERVED, THE MORE SUBSTANTIAL THE FOOD OFFERINGS.

THERE IS NO SUCH THING AS TRADITIONAL ENGLISH TEA COCKTAILS, SO YOU ARE FREE TO MAKE UP WHATEVER TRADITIONS SUIT YOUR FANCY. THIS COCKTAIL PAIRS DELIGHTFULLY WITH A SIMPLE BRUSCHETTA OR BAGELS AND LOX FOR BRUNCH.

1 pyramid tea bag or 1 teaspoon loose leaf Teatulia® White Tea
1 peach, cut into slices
8 fresh mint leaves
Juice from ¼ lemon
6 ice cubes
1 teaspoon honey simple syrup (page 124)
4 ounces bourbon

To make the tea, brew 1 tea bag or 1 teaspoon loose tea leaves in 8 ounces (about 1 mug) of hot water (just off the boil) for about 3 minutes. Remove tea bag or tea leaves and place brewed tea in the refrigerator to chill.

Set aside 2 thin peach slices and 2 mint leaves. Divide remaining peach slices, mint leaves, and lemon juice between 2 glasses and muddle to slightly mash the peaches. Add 2 ounces of brewed, chilled white tea, ice, honey simple syrup, and bourbon, and mix. Garnish with reserved peach slices and additional mint.

35

Rooibos Berry Daiquiri

Glass type: margarita or hurricane
Makes 2 cocktails

1 pyramid tea bag Teatulia® Rooibos Herbal Infusion
2 tablespoons honey simple syrup (page 124)
1 cup frozen strawberries or raspberries
1 cup ice cubes
4 ounces rum

To make the tea, brew 1 tea bag in 8 ounces (about 1 mug) of boiling water for about 5 minutes. Remove tea bag and place brewed tea in the refrigerator to chill.

Measure 4 ounces of the brewed, chilled tea and add to blender with remaining ingredients. Blend until smooth. Pour into 2 glasses and serve immediately.

Teatulia
ORGANIC TEAS

37

Rooibos Strawberry Mojito

Glass type: collins or pilsner
Makes 2 cocktails

1 pyramid tea bag Teatulia® Rooibos Herbal Infusion
4 strawberries, hulled and quartered
10 sprigs mint leaves, plus more for garnish
2 teaspoons simple syrup (page 123)
1 lime
4 ounces rum
½ cup club soda or seltzer
Crushed ice

Chill 2 glasses (each about 12 ounces).

To make the tea, brew 1 tea bag in 8 ounces (about 1 mug) of boiling water for about 5 minutes. Remove tea bag and place brewed tea in the refrigerator to chill.

Divide the strawberries, mint leaves, and simple syrup between the glasses and use the back of a spoon or a muddler to crush and mix together.

Squeeze ½ lime in each glass, divide the chilled tea and rum between the glasses, and stir. If using a shaker, shake together juice from the whole lime, tea, and rum, and pour between glasses. Top glasses off with crushed ice and club soda or seltzer. If desired, garnish with additional strawberry halves and mint leaves.

39

Green Tea and Grapefruit Cynar

Glass type: old fashioned or champagne flute

Makes 2 cocktails

CYNAR IS A BITTER ITALIAN LIQUEUR MADE FROM ARTICHOKES AND TWELVE OTHER HERBS AND PLANTS. YOU CAN SUBSTITUTE WITH BYRRH OR PUNT È MES, IF YOU HAPPEN TO HAVE EITHER OF THOSE ON HAND.

1 pyramid tea bag or 1 teaspoon loose leaf Teatulia®
* Green Tea*
1 ounce Cynar
4 ounces grapefruit juice
4 ounces chilled sparkling wine

   To make the tea, brew tea bag or loose leaf tea in 8 ounces (about 1 mug) of hot water (just off the boil) for about 3 minutes. Remove tea bag or leaves and place brewed tea in the refrigerator to chill.
   Measure 4 ounces of the chilled green tea. Divide the Cynar between 2 glasses and then add juice, tea, and sparkling wine. Serve immediately.

Teatulia
ORGANIC TEAS

41

Lavender White Tea Cocktail

Glass type: pilsner or hurricane

Makes 2 cocktails

THIS MIGHT BE THE PERFECT COCKTAIL FOR A BRIDAL SHOWER. AS PRETTY AS IT IS REFRESHING, IT WILL IMPRESS GUESTS AND MAKE FOR GORGEOUS PHOTOS. A QUICK SEARCH ONLINE YIELDS PLENTY OF PLACES YOU CAN PURCHASE DRIED LAVENDER.

2 cups water
2 teaspoons Teatulia® White Tea (or 2 pyramid tea bags)
2 tablespoons fresh or dried lavender flowers
2 tablespoons honey
4 ounces vodka
Additional lavender sprigs for garnish
Ice cubes

In a medium saucepan, heat the water to boiling and then remove from heat. Add tea, lavender flowers, and honey and allow to brew for at least 10 minutes. Remove tea, stir, strain, and chill. Place ice cubes in 2 glasses. In a shaker filled with ice, combine chilled tea and vodka and shake about 30 seconds. Strain into glasses and garnish with lavender sprigs.

"AS FAR AS HER MOM WAS CONCERNED, TEA FIXED EVERYTHING. HAVE A COLD? HAVE SOME TEA. BROKEN BONES? THERE'S A TEA FOR THAT TOO. SOMEWHERE IN HER MOTHER'S PANTRY, LAUREL SUSPECTED, WAS A BOX OF TEA THAT SAID, 'IN CASE OF ARMAGEDDON, STEEP THREE TO FIVE MINUTES.'"

—APRILYNNE PIKE, ILLUSIONS

43

Frozen Bloody Mary with Lemongrass

Glass type: pilsner

Makes 2 cocktails

*1 tea bag or 1 teaspoon loose leaf Teatulia®
  Lemongrass Herbal Infusion
2 cups cherry tomatoes, frozen
4 ounces vodka, chilled
Juice from 2 limes
1 teaspoon freshly grated horseradish
Coarse salt
Lemongrass stalk or celery stalk for garnish
  (optional)*

To make the tea, brew tea bag or loose leaf tea in 8 ounces (about 1 mug) of boiling water for about 5 minutes. Remove tea bag or leaves and place brewed tea in the refrigerator to chill.

Add all ingredients except salt and garnish to a blender and puree until smooth. Add salt to taste and divide between 2 glasses. Garnish with a stalk of lemongrass or celery.

45

Watermelon-Basil-White Tea Margarita Slushies

Glass type: margarita

Makes 2 cocktails

THIS DRINK IS SUMMER IN A GLASS. IF YOU'VE NEVER HAD BASIL IN A DRINK BEFORE, THIS IS A GREAT ONE TO START WITH—THE SWEETNESS OF THE WATERMELON MIXES WITH THE BOLD BASIL FLAVOR TO CREATE A DRINK THAT IS REFRESHING AND COMPLEX. CHOOSE SWEET BASIL, CINNAMON BASIL, LEMON BASIL, OR THAI BASIL DEPENDING ON WHAT'S AVAILABLE—ANY WILL BE DELICIOUS.

2 pounds watermelon, rind and seeds removed, cut into 1-inch squares
1 tea bag or 1 teaspoon loose leaf Teatulia® White Tea
2 teaspoons honey simple syrup (page 124)
3 ounces tequila
8 basil leaves, plus more for garnish
1 ounce triple sec

Line a baking sheet with parchment paper and place the watermelon cubes on it. Cover with another sheet of parchment paper and freeze for at least 2 hours.

To make the tea, brew tea bag or loose leaf tea in 8 ounces (about 1 mug) of hot water (just off the boil) for about 3 minutes. Remove tea bag or leaves and place brewed tea in the refrigerator to chill.

Combine frozen watermelon, chilled tea, and other ingredients in a blender and blend until slushy consistency. Divide between 2 glasses, garnish with basil leaves if desired, and serve.

47

Lemongrass Fizz

Glass type: old fashioned or pilsner
Makes 2 cocktails

1 pyramid tea bag or 1 teaspoons loose leaf Teatulia®
  Lemongrass Herbal Infusion
3 ounces vodka
2 ounces triple sec
3 teaspoons honey-ginger-lemon syrup (page 126)
½ cup crushed ice
4 ounces club soda
Lemon twists or slices, for garnish.

To make the tea, brew tea bag or loose leaf tea in 8 ounces (about 1 mug) of boiling water for about 5 minutes. Remove tea bag or leaves and place brewed tea in the refrigerator to chill.

In a shaker, combine vodka, triple sec, tea, honey-ginger-lemon syrup, and crushed ice and shake for about 30 seconds. Pour into 2 glasses and top off with club soda. Garnish with lemon twists or slices.

"DRINK IS THE FEAST OF REASON AND THE FLOW OF SOUL."

—ALEXANDER POPE

49

Herbal Ruby

Glass type: hurricane or martini
Makes 2 cocktails

1 pyramid tea bag Teatulia® Rooibos Herbal Infusion
1 tablespoon honey simple syrup (page 124)
2 ounces fresh ruby red grapefruit juice (juice from
   about ¼ grapefruit)
3 ounces vodka
3 sprigs fresh thyme or rosemary
2 ounces soda water

   To make the tea, brew tea bag in 8 ounces (about 1 mug) of boiling water for about 5 minutes. Remove tea bag and place brewed tea in the refrigerator to chill.
   In a shaker filled with ice, combine 4 ounces of chilled tea, simple syrup, grapefruit juice, vodka, and one sprig fresh rosemary. Shake for about 30 seconds and then strain into 2 glasses. Top off with soda water. Garnish with an additional sprig of rosemary in each glass.

Teatulia
ORGANIC TEAS

White Tea Punch

Glass type: punch glasses
Makes 8-10 cocktails

CREATED BY MIXOLOGIST ANIKA
ZAPPE FOR LINGER IN DENVER,
COLORADO. WWW.LINGERDENVER.COM

1 pyramid tea bag or 1 teaspoon loose leaf Teatulia®
  White Tea
6 ounces lemon juice
4 ounces simple syrup (page 123)
4 ounces Leopold Bros. peach liqueur
6 ounces St-Germain liqueur
8 ounces Boca Loca Cachaça
12 ounces Cava (or another dry sparkling wine)
5 dashes of Angostura bitters

To make the tea, brew in 8 ounces (about 1 mug) of hot
water (just off the boil) for about 3 minutes. Remove tea bag
and place brewed tea in the refrigerator to chill.
Combine chilled tea with remaining ingredients in a punch
bowl with a large ice block. Serve in punch glasses.

Teatulia
ORGANIC TEAS

White Tea Pimm's and Lemonade

Glass type: pilsner

Makes 2 cocktails

IF THERE'S ANYTHING MORE BRITISH THAN TEA, IT MIGHT BE PIMM'S. SIP AT A GARDEN PARTY OR, PREFERABLY, WHILE SITTING ON THE BANKS OF THE THAMES.

1 pyramid tea bag or 1 teaspoon loose leaf
  Teatulia® White Tea
2 slices cucumber, each about ½-inch thick
2 slices lemon
2 strawberries, hulled
4 ounces Pimm's No. 1
2 teaspoons honey-ginger-lemon syrup (page 126)
3 ounces soda water

To make the tea, brew in 8 ounces (about 1 mug) of hot water (just off the boil) for about 3 minutes. Remove tea bag or leaves and place brewed tea in the refrigerator to chill.

Place a cucumber slice, lemon slice, and strawberry in each glass and gently muddle. Add 3 ounces of chilled tea and remaining ingredients and stir to combine.

Blackberry and Black Tea Bourbon

Glass type: hurricane, old-fashioned, or pilsner

Makes 2 cocktails

1 pyramid tea bag or 1 teaspoon loose leaf Teatulia® Black Tea
¼ cup fresh blackberries
1 tablespoon sugar
1 tablespoon fresh chopped mint plus a few whole mint leaves for garnish
4 ounces bourbon
½ cup crushed ice

To make the tea, brew in 8 ounces (about 1 mug) of boiling water for about 3 minutes. Remove tea bag or leaves and place brewed tea in the refrigerator to chill.

In a small bowl, muddle the blackberries, sugar, and chopped mint and then divide between 2 glasses. In a shaker, combine the chilled tea, bourbon, and ice. Shake for about 30 seconds and then pour into glasses. Stir each glass lightly and then garnish with mint leaves.

55

Spiked Lemonade with Thyme

Glass type: collins, old fashioned, or pilsner
Makes 2 cocktails

2 cups water
¼ cup sugar
3 teaspoons loose leaf Ginger Herbal Infusion in a
   tea infuser (or 3 pyramid tea bags)
6-8 sprigs fresh thyme
4 ounces gin
¾ cup lemon juice
Crushed ice for serving

   Bring water to a boil, add sugar, and stir until dissolved.
Add tea and several sprigs of thyme, remove from heat, and
allow to steep for several minutes or until cool. Add gin
and lemon juice and stir. Place a little crushed ice in 2
glasses and pour mixture over. Serve with sprigs of thyme as
garnish.

57

Lemongrass Mojito

Glass type: collins or pilsner
Makes 2 cocktails

1 pyramid tea bag or 1 teaspoon loose leaf Teatulia®
  Lemongrass Herbal Infusion
2 stalks lemongrass
4 sprigs mint leaves
1 lime
4 ounces rum
2 tablespoons light brown sugar
¼ cup club soda or seltzer
¼ cup crushed ice

To make the tea, brew tea bag or leaves in 8 ounces (about 1 mug) of boiling water for about 5 minutes. Remove tea bag or leaves and place brewed tea in the refrigerator to chill.

Chill 2 glasses (each about 12 ounces). Finely chop the yellow, inner part of the lemongrass stalks. Divide lemongrass and mint leaves between glasses and use the back of a spoon or a muddler to crush and mix together.

Squeeze ½ lime in each glass, divide 4 ounces of chilled tea, rum, and sugar between the glasses, and stir. If using a shaker, shake together juice from the whole lime, tea, and rum, and pour between glasses. Top glasses off with crushed ice and club soda or seltzer. Garnish with additional lemongrass or mint leaves.

"ONE SIP OF THIS WILL BATHE THE DROOPING SPIRITS IN DELIGHT, BEYOND THE BLISS OF DREAMS."

—JOHN MILTON, COMUS

Frozen Mint Julep

Glass type: old fashioned or collins
Makes 2 cocktails

Traditionally, mint juleps are served in silver or pewter cups, but serve this frosty drink in whatever you like. To keep the flavor from diluting as the ice melts, use ice cubes made of peppermint tea.

1 pyramid tea bag or 1 teaspoon loose leaf Teatulia®
  Peppermint Herbal Infusion
6 ounces bourbon whiskey
3 teaspoons simple syrup (page 123)
10 fresh mint leaves
1½ cups crushed ice

   To make the tea, brew tea bag or leaves in 8 ounces (about 1 mug) of boiling water for about 5 minutes. Remove tea bag or leaves and place brewed tea in the refrigerator to chill.
   In a blender, combine bourbon, 4 ounces of chilled tea, simple syrup, and mint leaves and pulse until mint leaves are broken down into small bits. Add crushed ice and pulse until slushy. Pour into glasses and garnish with additional mint leaves.

01

Jasmine Green Tea Julep

Glass type: old fashioned or pilsner
Makes 2 cocktails

1 round tea bag Teatulia® Jasmine
  Green Tea
6 ounces bourbon whiskey
3 teaspoons simple syrup (page 123)
10 fresh mint leaves
6-8 ice cubes

   To make the tea, brew tea bag or leaves in 8 ounces (about 1 mug) of hot water (just off the boil) for about 3 minutes. Remove tea bag or leaves and place brewed tea in the refrigerator to chill.
   Divide mint leaves between 2 glasses and muddle gently. Add ice cubes. In a shaker filled with ice, combine 4 ounces of chilled tea with remaining ingredients and shake for about 30 seconds before straining into glasses.

63

Sweet and Spicy Cocktails

Rooibos Champagne

Glass type: champagne flutes
Makes 2 cocktails

ROOIBOS HAS A FLAVOR THAT'S
DIFFICULT TO DESCRIBE—A HINT OF
VANILLA WITH SMOKY UNDERTONES.
IT MAY SEEM TOO EARTHY TO PAIR
WITH CHAMPAGNE, THE CLASSIEST
OF DRINKS. BUT TOGETHER THEY
CREATE A COMPLEX, EFFERVESCENT
COCKTAIL PERFECT FOR YOUR MOST
SOPHISTICATED CELEBRATIONS.

1 pyramid tea bag Teatulia® Rooibos Herbal Infusion
6 ounces champagne, chilled

To make the tea, brew tea bag in 8 ounces (about 1 mug) of boiling water for about 5 minutes. Remove tea bag and place brewed tea in the refrigerator to chill.

Divide 6 ounces of chilled tea between 2 champagne flutes and then add champagne until the glasses are filled.

Ginger Lillet Sin

Glass type: old fashioned or hurricane
Makes 2 cocktails

LILLET IS A BRAND OF FRENCH
APERITIF WINE. IT CONTAINS
CINCHONA BARK, A SOURCE OF
QUININE, AND THUS IS CONSIDERED
A TONIC. COMBINED WITH THE GINGER,
LIME, AND FRESH MINT, THIS
COCKTAIL IS SURE TO CURE WHAT
"ALES" YOU.

1 pyramid tea bag or 1 teaspoon loose leaf Teatulia®
  Ginger Herbal Infusion
4 ounces Lillet Blanc
8 mint leaves
2 small wedges lime
2 teaspoons honey-ginger-lemon syrup (page 126)
2 ounces tonic water
6-8 ice cubes

To make the tea, brew tea bag or leaves in 8 ounces (about
1 mug) of boiling water for about 1 minute. Remove tea bag or
leaves and place brewed tea in the refrigerator to chill.
   Divide the mint and lime between 2 glasses and muddle
gently. Add ice cubes. In a cocktail shaker filled with ice,
shake 3 ounces of the chilled tea, honey-ginger-lemon syrup,
and Lillet Blanc. Strain into glasses and top off with tonic
water.

Green Tea Ginger Cooler

Glass type: pilsner
Makes 2 cocktails

THIS RECIPE, FROM ANIKA ZAPPE, WAS CREATED FOR LINGER, A POPULAR RESTAURANT AND LOUNGE IN DENVER, COLORADO THAT BOASTS A ROOFTOP PATIO AND A GLOBE-TROTTING MENU THAT FEATURES VEGAN AND GLUTEN-FREE DELIGHTS. LINGER. WWW.LINGERDENVER.COM.

1 pyramid tea bag or 1 teaspoon loose leaf Teatulia® Green Tea
1½ ounces lemon juice
1½ ounces simple syrup (page 123)
3 ounces Skyy ginger vodka

To make the tea, brew tea bag or leaves in 8 ounces (about 1 mug) of hot water (just off the boil) for about 3 minutes. Remove tea bag or leaves and place brewed tea in the refrigerator to chill.

Shake 4 ounces of chilled tea with remaining ingredients and ice. Strain and serve in 2 (12-ounce) glasses with fresh ice and a lemon wedge.

Rooibos Basil Refresher

Glass type: pilsner, margarita, or hurricane

Makes 2 cocktails

1 pyramid tea bag Teatulia® Rooibos Herbal Tea
2 ounces gin
3 teaspoons honey-ginger-lemon syrup (page 126)
6 basil leaves, torn
½ cup crushed ice
3 ounces club soda

To make the tea, brew tea bag or leaves in 8 ounces (about 1 mug) of boiling water for about 5 minutes. Remove tea bag or leaves and place brewed tea in the refrigerator to chill.

Place 3 ounces chilled tea in a shaker with the gin, syrup, basil leaves, and ice, and shake about 30 seconds. Pour into 2 glasses and top off with club soda.

71

Earl Grey Royal

Glass type: old fashioned
Makes 2 cocktails

EARL GREY TEA WAS NAMED AFTER A BRITISH PRIME MINISTER IN THE 1830S, THE 2ND EARL GREY. LEGEND HAS IT THAT THE SON OF A CHINESE BUREAUCRAT WAS RESCUED BY ONE OF LORD GREY'S MEN. THE FATHER PRESENTED THE EARL WITH TEA SCENTED WITH BERGAMOT OIL TO EXPRESS HIS GRATITUDE.

1 pyramid tea bag or 1 teaspoon loose leaf Teatulia®
  Earl Grey Tea
6-8 ice cubes
4 ounces gin
2 teaspoons honey simple syrup (page 124)
Juice from ½ orange (1-2 ounces)

To make the tea, brew tea bag or leaves in 8 ounces (about 1 mug) of boiling water for about 3 minutes. Remove tea bag or leaves and place brewed tea in the refrigerator to chill.

Fill 2 glasses halfway with ice cubes. Combine 4 ounces of chilled tea, gin, honey simple syrup, and orange juice in a cocktail shaker filled with ice. Shake for about 30 seconds and then strain into glasses. Garnish with strips of orange peel.

"ARTHUR BLINKED AT THE SCREENS AND FELT HE WAS MISSING SOMETHING IMPORTANT. SUDDENLY HE REALIZED WHAT IT WAS.

"'IS THERE ANY TEA ON THIS SPACESHIP?' HE ASKED."

—DOUGLAS ADAMS,
THE HITCHHIKER'S GUIDE TO THE GALAXY

73

Ginger Snap

Glass type: old fashioned or martini
Makes 2 cocktails

1 pyramid tea bag or 1 teaspoon loose leaf
   Teatulia® Ginger Herbal Infusion
2 ounces amaretto
½ teaspoon Angostura bitters
1 teaspoon honey-ginger-lemon syrup (page 126)
Pinch ground cinnamon

   To make the tea, brew tea bag or leaves in 8 ounces
(about 1 mug) of boiling water for about 1 minute.
Remove tea bag or leaves and place brewed tea in the
refrigerator to chill.
   Combine 4 ounces chilled tea with remaining
ingredients in an ice-filled cocktail shaker and
shake for about 30 seconds. Strain into 2 glasses.

"COME, GENTLEMEN, I HOPE WE SHALL DRINK DOWN ALL UNKINDNESS."

—WILLIAM SHAKESPEARE,
THE MERRY WIVES OF WINDSOR

75

Breakfast Cooler

Glass type: collins
Makes 2 cocktails

THIS RECIPE IS FROM KEVIN BURKE
AND WAS CREATED FOR COLT &
GRAY, A LOCALLY OWNED AND
OPERATED NEIGHBORHOOD
RESTAURANT IN DENVER, COLORADO.
WWW.COLTANDGRAY.COM.

1 pyramid tea bag or 1 teaspoon loose leaf
  Teatulia® Breakfast Tea
3 ounces Plymouth Gin
1 ounce Dolin Blanc Vermouth
½ ounce Ramazotti Amaro
½ ounce honey simple syrup (page 124)
½ ounce lemon juice
2 lemon wedges, for garnish

To make the tea, brew tea bag or leaves in 8 ounces (about 1 mug) of boiling water for about 3 minutes. Remove tea bag or leaves and place brewed tea in the refrigerator to chill.

Combine all ingredients except tea and lemon wedges in a cocktail shaker with ice. Shake and strain over new ice in 2 collins glasses. Top with 4 ounces chilled Teatulia Breakfast Tea. Garnish each glass with a lemon wedge.

Lemongrass Singapore Sling

Glass type: hurricane or pilsner

Makes 2 cocktails

1 pyramid tea bag or 1 teaspoon loose leaf Teatulia®
  Lemongrass Herbal Infusion
4-6 ice cubes
3 ounces gin
2 teaspoons honey-ginger-lemon syrup or grenadine
  (page 126 or 132)
1 teaspoon fresh lemon juice
1 ounce cherry brandy or Cherry Heering
3 ounces club soda
Stalk of lemongrass or maraschino cherries for
  garnish

   To make the tea, brew tea bag or leaves in 8 ounces (about 1 mug) of boiling water for about 5 minutes. Remove tea bag or leaves and place brewed tea in the refrigerator to chill.
   Divide ice cubes between 2 glasses. Combine gin, 3 ounces chilled tea, honey-ginger-lemon syrup or grenadine, lemon juice, and cherry brandy in a shaker filled with ice and shake for about 30 seconds. Pour into glasses and top off with club soda. Garnish with lemongrass or cherries and serve.

Basil Lemongrass Gimlet

Glass type: martini or old fashioned
Makes 2 cocktails

A close cousin of the daiquiri, a traditional gimlet is just gin or vodka, lime juice, a bit of simple syrup, and sometimes a spot of soda water. Adding the lemongrass tea and basil gives this refreshing drink a distinctly summery flavor.

1 pyramid tea bag or 1 teaspoon loose leaf Teatulia®
   Lemongrass Herbal Infusion
12 fresh basil leaves plus 2 for garnish
Juice from 1 lime
2 tablespoons honey simple syrup (page 124)
3 ounces gin
Ice

To make the tea, brew tea bag or leaves in 8 ounces (about 1 mug) of boiling water for about 5 minutes. Remove tea bag or leaves and place brewed tea in the refrigerator to chill.
   Place the 12 basil leaves in a cocktail shaker, add the lime juice, and muddle to release the basil oil. Add the chilled tea, simple syrup, gin, and ice, and shake. Strain into 2 glasses and garnish each with a basil leaf.

The Tequila Cilantro Cocktail

Glass type: pilsner
Makes 1 cocktail

THIS SPICY COCKTAIL IS CONTRIBUTED
BY TEATULIA ORGANIC TEAS LOVER CHEF
SARIG AGASI. ENJOY WITH YOUR
FAVORITE MEXICAN FOOD!

4 cilantro leaves
5 ounces blanco tequila
2 ounces lemongrass simple syrup (page 130)
½ ounce fresh lime juice
Jalapeño slice, for garnish

Muddle cilantro leaves with a splash of lime juice. Combine blanco tequila, lemongrass simple syrup, and remaining fresh lime juice in a shaker. Shake over ice and strain into a cocktail glass. Float a thin slice of jalapeño on the top.

The Fifth Element

Glass type: margarita or martini
Makes 2 cocktails

THIS RECIPE IS FROM THE KITCHEN BOULDER, A COMMUNITY BISTRO IN HISTORIC DOWNTOWN BOULDER, COLORADO. WWW.THEKITCHEN.COM.

2 ounces Spirit Hound gin
2 ounces Dolin Blanc Vermouth
1 ounce Chamomile Sage Syrup*
1 ounce lemon juice
2 sage leaves, for garnish

Combine all ingredients in a shaker, shake, and pour into 2 glasses. Float a sage leaf in each glass.

*Chamomile Sage Syrup: Combine 32 ounces simple syrup (page 123) with 10 Teatulia® Chamomile Herbal Infusion pyramid tea bags and 30 grams (about ½ cup) fresh sage leaves. Bring the mixture to a boil, remove from heat, and allow to steep overnight. Remove tea bags, strain, and pour into a resealable container, and refrigerate for up to 2 weeks.

Honey Tea Thyme

Glass type: pilsner
Makes 2 cocktails

THIS RECIPE IS FROM ANIKA ZAPPE AND WAS CREATED FOR LINGER IN DENVER, COLORADO.
WWW.LINGERDENVER.COM

1 pyramid tea bag or 1 teaspoon loose leaf Teatulia®
 Black Tea
1½ ounces Honey Thyme Syrup*
1½ ounces lemon juice
3 ounces Tennessee whiskey
2 fresh thyme sprigs
2 lemon twists, for garnish

To make the tea, brew tea bag or leaves in 8 ounces (about 1 mug) of boiling water for about 3 minutes. Remove tea bag or leaves and place brewed tea in the refrigerator to chill.
    Shake 3 ounces chilled tea with Honey Thyme Syrup, lemon juice, whiskey, 1 thyme sprig, and ice. Strain into 2 (12-ounce) glasses with fresh ice and garnish each with ½ thyme sprig and a lemon twist.

*Honey Thyme Syrup: In a small saucepan combine 1 cup honey, ½ cup water, and a small handful of fresh thyme sprigs. Simmer for 10-15 minutes and let cool, then strain.

"AYE, BUT TODAY'S RAIN IS TOMORROW'S WHISKEY."

—SCOTTISH PROVERB

Lemongrass Gingerini

Glass type: martini
Makes 2 cocktails

Simple and refreshing, using lemongrass tea rather than lemon juice lends the gingerini a subtler flavor and an asian flair. Pair it with spring rolls or sushi at a cocktail party.

1 pyramid tea bag or 1 teaspoon loose leaf Teatulia®
  Lemongrass Herbal Infusion
4 ounces gin
1 tablespoon honey-ginger-lemon syrup (page 126)
Lemon wedges, for garnish
Sugar for rimming glasses (optional)

To make the tea, brew tea bag or leaves in 8 ounces (about 1 mug) of boiling water for about 5 minutes. Remove tea bag or leaves and place brewed tea in the refrigerator to chill.
  If desired, rim 2 glasses with sugar. In a shaker filled with ice, combine 4 ounces chilled tea with the gin and honey-ginger-lemon syrup and shake for about 30 seconds. Strain into 2 glasses. Garnish with lemon wedges.

Teatulia
ORGANIC TEAS

85

Ginger Lemongrass Mai Tai

Glass type: hurricane or collins
Makes 2 cocktails

1 pyramid tea bag or 1 teaspoon loose leaf
   Teatulia® Lemongrass Herbal Infusion
1 pyramid tea bag or 1 teaspoon loose leaf
   Teatulia® Ginger Herbal Infusion
1 cup crushed ice
3 ounces light rum
1½ ounces dark rum
1 ounce orange curaçao
2 teaspoons honey-ginger-lemon syrup (page
   126) or dash grenadine (page 132)

   To make the tea, place the Lemongrass and the Ginger
tea bags or leaves together in 8 ounces (about 1 mug)
of boiling water for about 5 minutes. Remove tea bag
or leaves and place brewed tea in the refrigerator to
chill.
   Divide the crushed ice between 2 glasses. Fill a
cocktail shaker with ice cubes and shake 4 ounces of
chilled tea with remaining ingredients for about 30
seconds. Strain into glasses and serve.

"HONESTLY, IF YOU'RE GIVEN THE CHOICE BETWEEN ARMAGEDDON OR TEA, YOU DON'T SAY 'WHAT KIND OF TEA?'"

—NEIL GAIMAN

Peppermint Cosmo

Glass type: martini
Makes 2 cocktails

THE PERFECT DRINK FOR A HOLIDAY
PARTY, PEPPERMINT COSMOS LOOK
AND TASTE BRIGHT AND CHEERY.
IF THE FRUIT JUICE DOESN'T ADD
ENOUGH SWEETNESS FOR YOUR
PALATE, ADD A BIT OF PEPPERMINT
SIMPLE SYRUP (PAGE 131).

4 ounces vodka
1 pyramid tea bag or 1 teaspoon loose leaf Teatulia®
   Peppermint Herbal Infusion
2 ounces cranberry or pomegranate juice
Juice from ½ lime

To make the tea, brew tea bag or leaves in 8 ounces (about
1 mug) of boiling water for about 5 minutes. Remove tea bag
or leaves and place brewed tea in the refrigerator to chill.
   Fill a cocktail shaker with ice and add 4 ounces of chilled
tea with remaining ingredients. Shake until chilled (about
30 seconds). Strain into 2 martini glasses. If you prefer a
sweeter drink, add a dash of triple sec or peppermint simple
syrup (page 131).

Dark and Stormy with Ginger Tea

Glass type: old fashioned
Makes 2 cocktails

1 pyramid tea bag or 1 teaspoon loose leaf Teatulia®
  Ginger Herbal Infusion
6-8 ice cubes
½ lime
4 ounces dark rum
4 ounces ginger ale

To make the tea, brew tea bag or leaves in 8 ounces (about 1 mug) of boiling water for about 5 minutes. Remove tea bag or leaves and place brewed tea in the refrigerator to chill.
Divide the ice cubes between 2 glasses. Divide the lime half into 2 pieces and squeeze each over the ice in each glass. Drop the peels into the glasses. Divide 4 ounces of chilled tea and the remaining ingredients between the glasses and stir gently.

91

Queen's Tipple

Glass type: martini
Makes 2 cocktails

THIS RECIPE IS FROM KEVIN BURKE AND WAS CREATED FOR COLT & GRAY, A LOCALLY OWNED AND OPERATED NEIGHBORHOOD RESTAURANT IN DENVER, COLORADO. WWW.COLTANDGRAY.COM.

3 ounces Breakfast Gin*
1½ ounces dry vermouth
1 ounce honey simple syrup (page 124)
1 ounce lemon juice
1 ounce egg whites
Orange bitters (page 122)
Lemon twist, for garnish

In a shaker without ice, shake honey simple syrup, lemon juice, and egg whites to froth. Add gin, dry vermouth, and ice. Hard shake for 30 seconds, then strain into 2 glasses. Garnish with lemon twist and 2 drops orange bitters.

*Breakfast Gin: Place 3 ounces loose leaf Teatulia® Breakfast Tea in 1 liter of breakfast gin and allow to infuse for 30 minutes at room temperature. Strain out tea leaves and store Breakfast Gin in a clean bottle with a lid or stopper.

Jerez Tea

Glass type: collins
Makes 2 cocktails

This recipe is from Kevin Burke and was created for Colt & Gray, a locally owned and operated neighborhood restaurant in Denver, Colorado. www.coltandgray.com.

93

1 pyramid tea bag or 1 teaspoon loose leaf Teatulia®
  Green Tea
3 ounces Amontillado sherry
1½ ounces Grand Marnier
1 ounce Dolin Dry vermouth
2 lemon wedges and mint sprigs, for garnish

   To make the tea, brew tea bag or leaves in 8 ounces (about 1 mug) of hot water (just off the boil) for about 3 minutes. Remove tea bag or leaves and place brewed tea in the refrigerator to chill.
   Divide chilled tea and other ingredients over ice in two collins glasses, stirring to combine. Garnish each glass with a lemon wedge and mint sprig.

Ginger Tea Greyhound

Glass type: old fashioned

Makes 2 cocktails

TO MAKE THIS DRINK ESPECIALLY FESTIVE, USE PINK GRAPEFRUIT JUICE. FRESH-SQUEEZED IS ALWAYS BEST!

1 pyramid tea bag or 1 teaspoon loose leaf Teatulia®
   Ginger Herbal Infusion
Coarse sugar (optional)
6-8 ice cubes
4 ounces grapefruit juice
4 ounces vodka
Fresh thyme or grapefruit wedges for garnish

To make the tea, brew tea bag or leaves in 8 ounces (about 1 mug) of boiling water for about 1 minute. Remove tea bag or leaves and place brewed tea in the refrigerator to chill.
   If desired, rim the glasses with coarse sugar.
   Divide the ice between 2 glasses. Add 4 ounces of the chilled tea, the juice, and vodka, and stir. If using fresh grapefruit, be sure to squeeze the juice out through a strainer to catch any seeds. Garnish with thyme or grapefruit wedges

Teatulia
ORGANIC TEAS

Chai White Russian

Glass type: old fashioned
Makes 2 cocktails

2 cups whole milk (soy or almond milk can be substituted)
4 Teatulia® Chai Tea pyramid tea bags
2 tablespoons brown sugar
6-8 ice cubes
2 ounces Kahlúa
2 ounces vodka
Dash ground cinnamon

Heat the milk in a saucepan, stirring constantly. When bubbles begin rising to the surface, remove from heat and add tea bags and brown sugar, stirring until the brown sugar dissolves. Allow to steep for about 15 minutes or until the milk cools to room temperature.

Divide ice cubes between glasses and add half the Kahlúa and vodka to each glass. Pour the cooled chai-infused milk on top and stir to mix. Garnish with a dash of ground cinnamon.

Teatulia
ORGANIC TEAS

Rooibos Jack Rose

Glass type: martini

Makes 2 cocktails

TO REALLY IMPRESS, MAKE YOUR OWN
GRENADINE (SEE PAGE 132). IT'LL
TASTE BETTER THAN STORE-BOUGHT
GRENADINE AND MAKE YOUR
COCKTAIL RUBY RED.

1 pyramid tea bag Teatulia®
  Rooibos Herbal Infusion
4 ounces applejack
1 ounces fresh lemon juice
2 tablespoons grenadine (page 132)

To make the tea, brew tea bag in 8 ounces (about 1 mug) of boiling water for about 5 minutes. Remove tea bag and place brewed tea in the refrigerator to chill.

Combine 4 ounces chilled tea with remaining ingredients in a shaker filled with ice. Shake, and strain into 2 glasses.

Dark and Smoky Cocktails

Neem Nectar Old Fashioned

Glass type: old fashioned

Makes 2 cocktails

NEEM NECTAR TEA IS A MIX OF BLACK TEA LEAVES AND NEEM LEAVES. NEEM TREES ARE EVERGREENS THAT ARE NATIVE TO INDIA. WITH THEIR OWN NATURAL PESTICIDES, NEEM TREES ARE KNOWN FOR THEIR ANTISEPTIC AND MEDICINAL PROPERTIES. THE TEA HAS HINTS OF ORANGE RIND AND CARAMEL FLAVOR.

1 pyramid tea bag or 1 teaspoon loose leaf Teatulia®
   Neem Nectar Tea
2 sugar cubes
6 dashes Angostura bitters
2 strips lemon zest
2 orange wedges
Ice (preferably frozen Neem Nectar Tea)
4 ounces bourbon
Club soda
2 maraschino cherries

   To make the tea, brew tea bag or leaves in 8 ounces (about 1 mug) of boiling water for about 5 minutes. Remove tea bag or leaves and place brewed tea in the refrigerator to chill.
   Place a sugar cube, 3 dashes bitters, 2 ounces chilled tea, strip of lemon zest, and an orange wedge in the bottom of each glass. Muddle together until the sugar dissolves. Add ice and 2 ounces bourbon to each glass and top off with club soda and a cherry.

Teatulia
ORGANIC TEAS

Yerba Mate Smoky Martini

Glass type: martini
Makes 2 cocktails

YERBA MATE HAS A BOLD, SMOKY FLAVOR THAT IS A PERFECT MATCH FOR WHISKY. THE LEMON ADDS JUST A LITTLE BRIGHTNESS.

1 pyramid tea bag Teatulia®
  Yerba Mate Herbal Tea
4 ounces gin
Dash of Scotch whisky
2 lemon twists

To make the tea, brew tea bag in 8 ounces (about 1 mug) of boiling water for about 5 minutes. Remove tea bag or leaves and place brewed tea in the refrigerator to chill.

Combine 3 ounces chilled tea and remaining ingredients (except lemon twists) in a shaker filled with ice. Shake briefly and strain into 2 martini glasses. Rub a lemon twist along the rim of each glass and then hang one over each rim as garnish.

Neem Nectar Whiskey Sour

Glass type: old fashioned or collins
Makes 2 cocktails

1 pyramid tea bag or 1 teaspoon loose leaf Teatulia®
  Neem Nectar Tea
4-6 ice cubes
2 tablespoons honey-ginger-lemon syrup (page 126)
Juice from 1 medium lemon
3 ounces bourbon
Lemon wedges, for garnish

    To make the tea, brew tea bag or leaves in 8 ounces (about
1 mug) of boiling water for about 5 minutes. Remove tea bag
or leaves and place brewed tea in the refrigerator to chill.
    Divide ice cubes between glasses and then add 3 ounces
chilled tea and remaining ingredients to a shaker with ice,
shake, and strain into glasses. Garnish with lemon wedges.

103

Tulsi Negroni

Glass type: old fashioned
Makes 2 cocktails

TULSI, KNOWN AS HOLY BASIL, IS THE "QUEEN OF HERBS" IN AYURVEDA.

TULSI TEA HAS A SWEET AND SPICY FLAVOR WITH UNDERCURRENTS OF UNSWEETENED COCOA. COMBINED WITH THE SPIRITS, IT MAKES FOR A STRONG APERITIF WITH COMPLEXLY LAYERED FLAVORS.

1 pyramid tea bag or 1 teaspoon loose leaf strong-
    brewed Teatulia® Tulsi Infusion Tea
6-8 ice cubes
3 ounces Campari
2 ounces gin
1 ounce sweet vermouth
Orange peel, for garnish

To make the tea, brew tea bag or leaves in 8 ounces (about 1 mug) of boiling water for about 5 minutes. Remove tea bag or leaves and place brewed tea in the refrigerator to chill.
    Divide ice cubes between 2 glasses. Combine liquors and 3 ounces chilled tea in a shaker filled with ice, and pour into glasses. Garnish with orange peel.

Earl Grey Martini

105

2 teaspoons loose leaf Teatulia® Earl Grey Tea
  in a tea infuser (or 2 pyramid tea or round tea
  bags)
1 lemon, plus twists for garnish
1 ounce simple syrup
3 ounces gin

   To make the tea, brew tea leaves or bags in 8 ounces
(about 1 mug) of boiling water for about 5 minutes.
Remove tea bag or leaves and place brewed tea in the
refrigerator to chill.
   Combine chilled tea, juice from lemon, simple syrup,
and gin in a shaker with ice and strain into martini
glasses. Garnish with lemon twists.

Rooibos Martini

Glass type: martini
Makes 2 cocktails

1 pyramid tea bag Teatulia® Rooibos Herbal
   Infusion
2 teaspoons honey simple syrup (page 124)
4 ounces vodka

   To make the tea, brew tea bag in 8 ounces (about 1 mug) of boiling water for about 5 minutes. Remove tea bag and place brewed tea in the refrigerator to chill.
   Combine chilled tea, honey simple syrup, and vodka in a shaker with ice and strain into martini glasses.

Lapsang Manhattan

Glass type: martini
Makes 2 cocktails

THIS RECIPE IS FROM KEVIN BURKE AND WAS CREATED FOR COLT & GRAY, A LOCALLY OWNED AND OPERATED NEIGHBORHOOD RESTAURANT IN DENVER, COLORADO. WWW.COLTANDGRAY.COM.

3½ ounces Sazerac 6-year rye whiskey
*2 ounces Black Tea Vermouth**
½ ounce Luxardo Maraschino liqueur
Lemon bitters
Dash Laphroaig 10-year Scotch whisky (any smoky whisky will do)
2 lemon twists, for garnish

Combine rye, whiskey, Black Tea Vermouth, Maraschino, and bitters over ice in a stirring glass. Stir 20 seconds to chill. Add Scotch whisky and then divide between 2 glasses. Garnish with a lemon twist on each glass.

*Black Tea Vermouth: Combine 3 ounces of loose leaf Teatulia® Black Tea with 750mL of Dolin Rosso Vermouth. Let rest for 30 minutes. Strain out tea leaves and pour into a clean container with a lid or stopper.

Teatulia
ORGANIC TEAS

Tulsi and Rye

Glass type: old fashioned
Makes 2 cocktails

1 pyramid tea bag or 1 teaspoon loose leaf
  Teatulia® Tulsi Infusion Tea
2 teaspoons simple syrup (page 123)
6 dashes Angostura bitters
1 teaspoon fresh lemon juice
4 ounces rye whiskey
Ice (preferably frozen Tulsi Infusion Tea cubes)
Lemon peel, for garnish

109

To make the tea, brew tea bag or leaves in 8 ounces (about 1 mug) of boiling water for about 5 minutes. Remove tea bag or leaves and place brewed tea in the refrigerator to chill.

In a cocktail shaker combine chilled tea and remaining ingredients (except lemon peel) and shake for about 30 seconds. Pour into old fashioned glasses and garnish with twists of lemon peel.

Warm and Toasty Cocktails

Ginger Glögg

Glass type: mug
Makes 12 cocktails

1 bottle red wine
3 tablespoons orange zest
2 cinnamon sticks
10 whole cardamom seeds
10 whole cloves
4 pyramid tea bags or 4 teaspoons loose leaf Teatulia®
    Ginger Herbal Infusion
½ cup honey
½ pound raisins (optional)
3 ounces brandy

   Pour wine into a large pot. Place orange zest, cinnamon
sticks, cardamom seeds, and cloves in a square of
cheesecloth, form a little pouch, and tie with kitchen
string. Add to wine, along with the tea bags or leaves
(in an infuser). Boil for about 15 minutes, add honey and
raisins (if using) and boil another 15 minutes, stirring
occasionally. Remove spice pouch and tea bags or infuser,
add brandy, stir, and serve hot.

Swedish Toddy

Glass type: mug
Makes 2 cocktails

THIS RECIPE IS FROM KEVIN BURKE AND WAS CREATED FOR COLT & GRAY, A LOCALLY OWNED AND OPERATED NEIGHBORHOOD RESTAURANT IN DENVER, COLORADO. WWW.COLTANDGRAY.COM.

1 pyramid tea bag or 1 teaspoon loose leaf Teatulia®
  Tulsi Infusion Tea
1 teaspoon honey
2 ounces aquavit (Krogstad or O.P. Anderson)
Star anise
Lemon twist

113

To make the tea, brew tea bag or leaves in 8 ounces (about 1 mug) of boiling water for about 5 minutes. Remove tea bag or leaves.

Dissolve honey in hot tea and add aquavit. Divide between 2 glasses and garnish with lemon twists and star anise.

Ginger Mulled Cider

Glass type: mug

Makes 6 servings

IS THERE ANYTHING MORE FESTIVE ON A FALL EVENING THAN HOT MULLED CIDER? THE GINGER TEA MAKES THE CIDER EVEN MORE WARMING, AND YOUR KITCHEN WILL SMELL FANTASTIC AS THE DRINK SIMMERS ON YOUR STOVETOP.

1 pint cider
2 ounces dark rum
3 teaspoons loose leaf Teatulia® Ginger Herbal
  Infusion in a tea infuser (or 3 pyramid tea bags)
2 tablespoons brown sugar
6 whole cloves
2 cinnamon sticks
2 cardamom pods (optional)

Combine all ingredients in a large saucepan and heat to near boiling. Simmer for 20-30 minutes. Remove tea bags or tea infuser and ladle into mugs to serve.

Teatulia
ORGANIC TEAS

Earl Grey Cream Tea

Glass type: old fashioned
Makes 2 cocktails

BENEDICTINE IS A SWEET HERBAL LIQUOR. AS A SUBSTITUTE, YOU CAN USE BRANDY AND DISSOLVE A TABLESPOON OF HONEY IN THE HOT MILK.

2 cups milk
2 teaspoons loose leaf Teatulia® Earl Grey Tea in a
*   tea infuser (or 2 pyramid or round tea bags)*
3 ounces Benedictine

In a medium saucepan, heat the milk, stirring constantly, until bubbles begin to rise to the surface. Add tea, remove from heat, and allow to steep, covered, for about five minutes. Remove tea bags or tea infuser. If tea has cooled too much, heat again. If a thin skin has formed at the top of the milk, remove and discard. Add Benedictine, stir, and divide between 2 mugs. This drink can also be served chilled over ice.

Riesling Jasmine Hot Toddy

Glass type: mug
Makes 4 drinks

1 (750 milliliter) bottle Riesling wine
2 teaspoons brandy
3 Teatulia® Jasmine Green Tea round tea bags
Juice from 1 lemon
2 tablespoons honey

In a saucepan, combine all ingredients and simmer for about 10 minutes, stirring occasionally. Remove tea bags and simmer another 20 minutes. Ladle into mugs and serve hot.

Teatulia
ORGANIC TEAS

Hot Earl Grey and Bourbon

Glass type: mug
Makes 2 cocktails

1 pyramid tea bag or 1 teaspoon loose leaf Teatulia®
   Earl Grey tea
1 teaspoon honey
3 ounces bourbon
2 teaspoons cream

To make the tea, brew tea bag or leaves in 8 ounces (about 1 mug) of boiling water for about 3 minutes.
While the tea is hot, add the honey and stir to dissolve. Divide between 2 mugs and add bourbon and cream. Serve hot.

Chai Latte Hot Buttered Rum

Glass type: mug
Makes 4 cocktails

Think putting butter in a cocktail is weird? Tibetans enjoy a savory "butter tea," made from black tea, yak butter, and salt. You could dump a shot glass of whiskey in there and make it a cocktail, but yak butter is tough to find in most of the world. Chai Latte Hot Buttered Rum is creamy and sweet and perfect served by the fireplace on a cold night.

2 pyramid tea bags Teatulia® Chai Tea
⅔ cup dark brown sugar
½ cup unsalted butter, softened
¼ cup honey
½ teaspoon ground cinnamon
¼ teaspoon ground nutmeg
2 cups warm milk
8 ounces spiced rum
4 cinnamon sticks (for garnish)

To make the tea, brew tea bags in 8 ounces (about 1 mug) of boiling water for about 3 minutes.

In a blender or food processor, blend together the brown sugar, butter, honey, cinnamon, and nutmeg. Add the warm milk, rum, and hot chai tea and blend until frothy. Pour into 4 cups, place a cinnamon stick in each, and serve.

119

Homemade Bitters and Simple Syrups

Simple Orange Bitters

Makes 1 pint

Peels from four oranges
2 cups Everclear 151 or high proof vodka (at least
* 100 proof)*
½ teaspoon fennel seed
¼ teaspoon ground coriander
4 cardamom pods, cracked
6 whole cloves

Dry the orange peels in a food dehydrator or in the oven set to 175 degrees Fahrenheit for 2 hours. Place the dried orange peels in a quart-size glass jar and pour the alcohol over the peels. Add spices, cover jar tightly with lid, and place in a cool, dark area. Shake the bottle once a day for about 2 weeks. Taste the mixture. If it's the flavor you want, strain out the solids through cheesecloth and return the liquid to the jar. For stronger bitters, leave the orange peels and spices in longer. Bitters can be stored without refrigeration for years but will taste best if used within a year.

Simple Syrup

Makes about 1 cup

1 cup water
1 cup sugar

Combine ingredients in a small saucepan and bring to a boil. Simmer for about 5 minutes. Remove from heat and allow to cool. Store in a covered glass container in the refrigerator for up to a month.

123

Honey Simple Syrup

Makes 1 cup

1 cup honey
1 cup water

    In a small saucepan, combine honey and water and heat, stirring, until honey dissolves. Allow to cool completely. Store in a covered glass container in the refrigerator for up to a month.

125

Honey-Ginger-Lemon Syrup

Makes ½ cup

THIS SYRUP ADDS A BRIGHT CITRUS
FLAVOR TO YOUR MIXED DRINKS. YOU CAN
ALSO MIX IT WITH SELTZER TO MAKE YOUR
OWN GINGER ALE.

Juice from 1 lemon
½ cup honey
½ cup water
4 tablespoons freshly grated ginger

   Combine ingredients in a small saucepan and bring to a
boil. Simmer for about 5 minutes. Strain through a fine mesh
strainer and use immediately or store in a covered glass
container in the refrigerator for up to a month.

127

Maple Simple Syrup

Makes 1 cup

1 cup pure maple syrup
1 cup water

In a small saucepan, combine maple syrup and water and heat, stirring, until maple syrup dissolves. Allow to cool completely. Store in a covered glass container in the refrigerator for up to a month.

Coconut Sugar Simple Syrup

Makes ⅓ cup

1 cup coconut sugar
⅓ cup water

129

In a small saucepan, heat the coconut sugar and water, stirring until sugar is fully dissolved. Remove from heat and allow to cool to room temperature. Store in a covered glass container in the refrigerator for up to a month.

Lemongrass Simple Syrup

Makes 2 cups

2 teaspoons loose leaf Teatulia® Lemongrass Herbal Infusion (or 2 pyramid or round tea bags)
2 cups water
1½ cups honey or ¾ cup sugar

Boil the water, add tea and honey or sugar, and stir until honey or sugar is fully dissolved. Remove from heat and allow tea to steep until water cools to room temperature. Remove tea infuser or tea bags and store syrup in a covered glass container in the refrigerator for up to a month.

Teatulia
ORGANIC TEAS

Peppermint Simple Syrup

Makes 2 cups

2 Teatulia® Peppermint Herbal Infusion tea bags (or 2
  teaspoons of loose leaf Peppermint Herbal Infusion
  in a tea infuser)
2 cups water
1½ cups honey or ¾ cup sugar

Boil the water, add tea bags and honey or sugar, and stir until honey or sugar is fully dissolved. Remove from heat and allow tea to steep until water cools to room temperature. Remove tea bags or tea infuser and store syrup in a covered glass container in the refrigerator for up to a month.

Simple Grenadine

Makes 1½ cups

2 cups pomegranate juice (no sugar added)
1 cup granulated sugar
Dash orange flower water (optional)

Combine pomegranate juice and sugar in a saucepan and bring to a slow boil, stirring occasionally for about 10 minutes. Remove from heat and allow to cool. Add orange flower water, if using, and stir. Store in a sealed glass bottle in the refrigerator for a few weeks, or add a tablespoon of high-proof vodka to increase the shelf life.

133

Tea-infused Appetizers

Bacon-Wrapped Dates with Coconut Chai Dipping Sauce

Makes 18

THIS RECIPE IS ADAPTED FROM PETITE EATS BY TIMOTHY LAWRENCE.

20 medjool dates
9 bacon strips, sliced in half
1 tablespoon butter
½ can coconut milk
2 tablespoons maple syrup
2 Teatulia® Chai pyramid tea bags
1 tablespoon all-purpose flour
½ teaspoon salt
⅛ cup water

Wrap 18 dates (set two aside for use in the sauce) in bacon and skewer each with a toothpick. Place on baking sheet. Bake in preheated, 350 degree oven for 20-25 minutes or until bacon is crisp. Remove and let cool about 10 minutes before serving.

While dates are cooking, prepare sauce. Cut two dates in half. Sauté in butter until butter browns slightly. Add coconut milk, maple syrup, and tea bags. Let simmer 10 minutes. Remove from heat and take out date halves and tea bags.

Mix flour and salt in ⅛ cup cold water until dissolved. Mix with coconut chai sauce to thicken. If sauce is still runny, return to heat and simmer until thickened.

Grilled Zucchini with a Tulsi Rub

Makes 3-4 servings

TULSI RUB
2 tablespoons loose leaf Teatulia® Tulsi
    Infusion Tea
1 tablespoon sea salt
½ teaspoon dried thyme
¼ teaspoon black pepper

1 zucchini
Olive oil (for brushing)
Goat cheese

   To make the rub, combine all ingredients in a spice grinder.
   Wash the zucchini and cut into strips that are the length of the zucchini and about ¼-inch thick. While the grill is heating, brush both sides of the zucchini strips with olive oil and dip in the tulsi rub to coat.
   Grill until zucchini is tender-crisp (about 8-12 minutes), turning occasionally. Transfer zucchini from grill to a cutting board and cut into 2" pieces. Place a small dollop of goat cheese on each piece and serve.

Summer Rolls with Green Tea Dipping Sauce

Makes 5 rolls

SUMMER ROLLS
10 rice paper rounds (6- or 8-inches in diameter)
5 lettuce leaves
1 carrot, coarsely shredded
Small bunch fresh cilantro
Small bunch fresh mint
1 Haas avocado, halved, pitted, and cut into thin
  wedges

DIPPING SAUCE
1 pyramid tea bag or 1 teaspoon loose leaf Teatulia®
  Green Tea
2 tablespoons grapeseed oil
1 tablespoon unfiltered apple cider vinegar
2 tablespoons honey
1 tablespoon tamari
½ teaspoon salt

To make the tea, brew tea bag or leaves in 8 ounces (about 1 mug) of hot water (just off the boil) for about 3 minutes. Remove tea bag or leaves and place brewed tea in the refrigerator to chill.

Fill a pie plate with warm water and lay a towel flat on the work surface beside it. Dip one rice paper round in the warm water and allow to soften for a few seconds. Remove and lay flat on the towel. Repeat with a second round, laying it directly on top of the first rice paper round. Pat the top dry with a paper towel.

Place a lettuce leaf sideways across the bottom third of the rice paper. Arrange the carrot, avocado, and a few leaves of the cilantro and mint in a neat row beside the lettuce, leaving about an inch of space around the edges. Fold in the sides and then roll up the whole thing into a log. Slice in half and serve with dipping sauce.

To make the sauce, whisk together 4 ounces of the chilled tea along with the other ingredients and serve in a shallow bowl alongside summer rolls.

139

Yerba Mate-infused Chicken Salad Cups

Makes 6-8 salad cups

THIS RECIPE IS ADAPTED FROM "CHICKEN SALAD LETTUCE CUPS" IN *PETITE EATS* BY TIMOTHY LAWRENCE. THE YERBA MATE ADDS A SUBTLE SMOKY FLAVOR TO THE CHICKEN, WHICH IS BALANCED BY THE TART CRANBERRIES.

1 boneless, skinless chicken breast
2 pyramid tea bags Teatulia® Yerba Mate Herbal Infusion
1 tablespoon mayonnaise
1 tablespoon chopped pecans
1 tablespoon chopped dried cranberries
Salt and pepper to taste
¼ (a wedge) iceberg lettuce

Poach chicken breast: Place in a saucepan and add water so that it covers the chicken by at least half an inch. Bring to a boil, reduce heat, cover pot, and simmer for about 5 minutes. Add tea bags and simmer an additional 5 minutes. Turn off the heat, remove the tea bags, and allow chicken to keep cooking in hot tea for another 10 to 15 minutes.

Remove chicken from poaching water and dice. Mix with mayonnaise, chopped pecans, chopped cranberries, and salt and pepper.

Fill individual leaves of lettuce with chicken salad. If lettuce cups are sagging, skewer with a toothpick to hold in place.

Shrimp with Bloody Mary Cocktail Sauce

Makes 4-6 servings

THIS BLOODY MARY COCKTAIL SAUCE IS ESSENTIALLY THE SAME RECIPE USED TO MAKE THE FROZEN BLOODY MARY WITH LEMONGRASS COCKTAILS (PAGE 44), EXCEPT WITH A LITTLE LESS LIQUID.

1 pound large cooked and peeled shrimp

BLOODY MARY COCKTAIL SAUCE
2 cups cherry tomatoes, frozen
3 ounces vodka, chilled
Juice from 2 limes
1 teaspoon freshly grated horseradish
1 pyramid tea bag or 1 teaspoon loose leaf
  Teatulia® Lemongrass Herbal Infusion
Coarse salt to taste

   To make the tea, brew tea bag or leaves in 8 ounces (about 1 mug) of boiling water for about 5 minutes. Remove tea bag or leaves and place brewed tea in the refrigerator to chill.
   To make the cocktail sauce, combine 6 ounces chilled tea with remaining ingredients in a blender and pulse until smooth but not too liquidy. Pour into a shallow bowl, arrange shrimp around the outside, and serve immediately.

Caprese Skewers with Lemongrass Tea Dipping Sauce

Makes 18

FOR THE CAPRESE SKEWERS
9 Cherry tomatoes
18 Mozzarella balls
18 fresh basil leaves

FOR THE DIPPING SAUCE
1 pyramid tea bag or 1 teaspoon loose leaf
  Teatulia® Lemongrass Herbal Infusion
2 tablespoons grapeseed oil
1 tablespoon white vinegar
2 tablespoons honey
1 tablespoon lemon juice
½ teaspoon salt

Slice cherry tomatoes in half. Deseed if desired and remove stems. Skewer one piece of tomato, one mozzarella ball, and one basil leaf on each toothpick and repeat until you've made desired number.

To make the tea, place the Lemongrass tea bags or leaves in 8 ounces (about 1 mug) of boiling water for about 5 minutes. Remove tea bag or leaves and place brewed tea in the refrigerator to chill. To make the dipping sauce, combine 4 ounces of chilled tea with remaining ingredients in a food processor or shake in a jar. Serve in a small bowl alongside the caprese skewers.

143

Tea Glossary

HARVESTING AND PRODUCTION TERMS

CAMELLIA SINENSIS: The species of plant whose leaves are used to produce tea. Black, green, white, oolong, and pu-erh teas all come from this plant. There are two varietals: *C. Sinensis sinensis* and *C. Sinensis assamica*.

CTC: Cut-Tear-Curl method of tea processing resulting in broken leaves.

FAIR TRADE: Program run by Trans Fair International intended to provide growers with a fair price for their teas.

GARDEN/ESTATE: Farm or plantation that grows tea of varying scale and scope.

GARDEN-DIRECT: Teas that come to the marketplace directly from the garden of origin without being handled by brokers or distributors.

GRADES: Terms used to describe black teas from the Indian subcontinent, Indonesia, and Africa and are based on the size of the leaf and the presence of tips. Tippy, golden, flowery, broken, orange pekoe are some of the grading terms used and are usually abbreviated (e.g. OP, BOP, FOP, GFOP, TGFOP, etc.)

FLUSH: A complete group or complement of fully-developed tea leaves ready for harvest plucking. The unopened bud and next two leaves are harvested.

ORGANIC: Teas grown with a strict adherence to agricultural guidelines for natural cultivation set by the USDA and other national certifying bodies.

ORGANOLEPTIC: The ability of tea to make an impression on the senses of taste, smell, sight, and viscosity within the mouth.

ORIGIN: Typical tea origins include India, Sri Lanka (Ceylon), China, and Japan. More recent origins include Bangladesh, Vietnam, and parts of Africa.

ORTHODOX: Whole leaf tea.

PLUCK: To pick or harvest tea.

SINGLE-GARDEN: From one tea garden or estate rather than multiple gardens. Most commercially available teas are a blend of teas from multiple gardens.

TISANES: Herbal infusions not derived from the *Camellia sinensis* plant.

SPECIFIC TERMS USED TO DESCRIBE DRY LEAVES

BLACKISH: This is satisfactory appearance for CTC manufacture teas and denotes careful sorting.

BLOOM: A "sheen" which has not been removed due to over-handling or over-sorting. It is a sign of good manufacture and sorting (where the reduction of leaf has taken place before firing).

BOLD: Particles of leaf, which are too large for the particular grade.

BROKEN: Tea with many small or broken pieces of leaves.

BROWN: A brown appearance, with CTC manufacture, normally reflects too harsh treatment of the leaf.

CHESTY: A taint caused by inferior or unseasoned packing materials.

CHOPPY: Orthodox manufacture leaf that needs to be cut by a "breaker" during sorting.

CHUNKY: A very large broken leaf that results from orthodox manufacture.

CLEAN: Free from fiber, dust, and any extraneous matter.

CREPEY: A crimped appearance from orthodox manufacture common with larger grades of broken leaf tea such as BOP.

CURLY: The leaf appearance of whole leaf grade Orthodox teas such as OP. The opposite of wiry.

EVEN: Size is true to grade and of consistent size.

FANNINGS/DUST: The tiny bits and pieces, usually leftovers from processing. Commonly found in conventional paper tea bags.

FIBER: Shreds of stalk found in dry leaves—indicating bad particles.

FLAKEY: Flat, open, and often light in texture.

GOLDEN TIPS: The desirable golden tip of the smallest, most tender leaves.

GREY: Caused by too much abrasion during sorting.

GRAINY: Describes well-made CTC primary grades, particularly Pekoe Dust and Dust 1 grades.

IRREGULAR: Uneven pieces of leaf in whole-leaf grades resulting from inadequate or poor sorting.

LEAFY: Orthodox manufacture leaf tending to be on the large or long side.

LIGHT: A tea light in weight and of poor density. Sometimes referred to as flaky.

MAKE: A well made tea (or not) and must be true to the particular grade.

MUSHY/MUSTY: A tea that has been packed or stored with a high moisture content.

NEAT: A grade having good "make" and size.

NOSE: Smell of the dry leaf.

OPEN: Opposed to twisted—unrolled.

POWDERY: A fine light dust.

RAGGED: An uneven or poorly manufactured and graded tea.

STALK & FIBER: Parts of the tea plant that should be minimal in primary or top grades but generally acceptable in the lower grades.

TIP: A sign of fine plucking and apparent in the top grades of Orthodox manufacture.

UNEVEN & MIXED: "Inconsistent" pieces of leaf indicating poor sorting and untrue to the particular grade of tea.

WELL-TWISTED: Applies to Orthodox manufacture. Often referred to as "well made" or "rolled" and used to describe whole leaf grades.

WIRY: The appearance of a well-twisted, thin leaf Orthodox tea.

GENERAL TERMS

AGONY OF THE LEAVES: Unfolding of the tea leaves in hot water.

AROMA: Smell or "nose" denoting "inherent character."

AUTUMNAL: A term used to describe the earthy, fuller-flavors characteristic of fall tea crops.

BAKEY: A over-fired tea in which too much moisture has been driven off.

BODY: A tactile sensation related to tea viscosity and strength of liquor combined with weight on the tongue. Body can be wispy, light, medium, or full. Also called "mouth feel."

CHARACTER: Intrinsic traits of the tea liquor, broadly identifying a tea by country, region, or estate.

COLOR: The color of brewed liquor is determined by country, district, varietal, harvest conditions, processing methods, and preparation. For example, black tea tends to be reddish, oolong is brown to greenish-yellow, green tea is pale green, and white tea sometimes has a nice pinkish hue.

FINISH: A measure of the taste or flavors that linger in the mouth after the tea is tasted.

FLAVOR: A most desirable extension of "character."

LIQUOR: The brewed tea liquid that remains when leaves are removed after steeping.

NOSE: The aroma and essence emitted by brewed tea liquor and fresh or dried leaves.

PEAK: The high point of a cupping experience—when the liquor enters the mouth and its body, flavor, and astringency make themselves fully felt in combination.

QUALITY: Refers to "cup quality" and denotes a combination of the most desirable liquoring propertics.

STRENGTH: The measure of the substance in a cup.

TANNIN: A vital chemical component of tea that is responsible for its astringent, palate-cleansing character.

DESIRABLE FLAVOR CHARACTERISTICS

BRIGHT: Denotes a lively fresh tea with good keeping quality.

BRISK: A lively taste in the liquor, without being too high in bitter tannins, as opposed to flat or soft.

CLEAN: Fresh on the palate and free of any off-taste.

COMPLEX: A term that describes integration of aromatic and flavor components in finer-quality teas, referring to a tea's display of multi-dimensional layers.

COPPERY: Bright leaf, which indicates a well-manufactured tea.

EARTHY: Describes teas with aromas or flavors of soil or earth.

FULL-BODIED: A good combination of strength and color.

GRASSY: A somewhat raw, hay-like flavor often associated with greens and some oolongs.

HARD: A very pungent liquor.

HIGH-FIRED: Over-fired but not bakey or burnt.

MALTY: A subtle underlying flavor often characteristic of Assams.

MATURE: Not bitter or flat.

MELLOW: Smooth, easy, and pleasant. The opposite of harsh or greenish.

MUSCATEL: A term traditionally used in reference to a sweet varietal of white wine but is used in the tea world to describe the classic characteristic flavors of brewed Darjeeling liquor.

PUNGENT: Astringent with a good combination of briskness, brightness, and strength. Often reserved for the best quality Assam and Ceylon teas.

SELF-DRINKING: Any tea with sufficient aroma, flavor, body, and color to stand alone, with no need of blending (when dry) or condiments (after brewing) to improve drinkability.

SMOOTH: A liquor with a rounded taste and body that is pleasant to the palate.

SOFT: The opposite of briskness and lacking any "live" characteristics.

TARRY: A smoky aroma.

UNDESIRABLE FLAVOR CHARACTERISTICS

BAKEY: An over-fired tea in which too much moisture has been driven off.

BRASSY: Liquor with a strong, bitter taste.

BURNT: Off color and flavor caused by extreme over-firing.

COARSE: The taste of the liquor has a rough quality (bitterness or too much acidity) due to improper processing, such as the inclusion of too much fiber.

COMMON: A very plain tea, light and thin liquor with no distinct flavor.

CREAM/CLOUDING: A precipitate obtained after cooling.

DARK: A dark or dull color, which indicates a poor quality leaf.

DRY: Indicates slight over-firing.

DULL: Tea with a muddy liquor that lacks brightness or briskness. Also describes a leaf without sheen or brilliance.

FLAT: Off or stale taste.

FRUITY: Can be due to over-oxidization or bacterial infestation before firing, delivering an overly ripe taste. Also positively associated with good oolongs.

GREEN: An immature "raw" character. Often due to under-fermentation and/or under-withering.

HARD: A very pungent liquor.

HARSH: A rough taste generally related to under-withered leaves.

HEAVY: A thick, strong, and deep-colored liquor with limited briskness. Similar attributes to full-bodied tea, but taken to excess.

LIGHT: Lacking strength and any depth of color. Also known as wispy.

METALLIC: A sharp coppery flavor.

MIXED/DISTORTED/UNEVEN: Tea leaves of varying color.

MUDDY: A dull opaque liquor.

OFF/GONE OFF: A flat or otherwise bad tea often due to a high moisture content.

PLAIN: A liquor which is "clean" but lacking in the desirable characteristics.

POINT: A bright, acidy, and penetrating characteristic.

RASPING: A very course and harsh liquor.

RAW: A bitter, tart, tangy, rough, super-grassy, or overall unpleasant liquor.

STEWED: A soft liquor with an undesirable taste caused by faulty firing at low temperatures and often insufficient air flow.

TAINTS: Characteristics (or tastes) which are "foreign" to tea, caused by improper storage and shipping. Taints can include petrol, spices, coffee, etc.

THIN: An insipid light liquor which lacks any desirable characteristics.

WEEDY: A grass or hay taste related to under-withering. Sometimes referred to as woody.

WISPY: Liquor that is lacking in both strength and depth of color.

Sources

History of Business. "History of Lipton Tea." http://
historyofbusiness.blogspot.com/2012/05/history-of-lipton-tea.
html (accessed July 2014).

Mary Lou and Robert J. Heiss, *The Story of Tea: A Cultural History and Drinking Guide*. California: Ten Speed Press, 2007.

Mayo Clinic. "Nutrition and Healthy Eating." http://www.
mayoclinic.org/healthyliving/nutrition-and-healthy-eating/
multimedia/antioxidants/sls-20076428 (accessed July 2014).

School of Tea. "Tea Manufacturing Process." http://www.
schooloftea.org/teamanufacturing-process/ (accessed 2014).

Tea Answers. "51 Tea Facts Every Tea Lover Should Know." http://
www.teaanswers.com/tea-facts-trivia/ (accessed July 2014).

Teatulia Organic Tea. "Tea 101." http://www.teatulia.com (accessed
July 2014).

Teekanne. "The History of the Tea Bag." http://www.teekanne.com/
about-teainfusions/history/tea-bags/ (accessed July 2014).

Tetley. "A (Tea) Potted History." http://www.tetley.com.mt/about-us/
history (accessed July 2014).

The Free Library. "Brooke Bond's 'Gotta Brand New Bag.'" http://
www.thefreelibrary.com/Brooke+Bond%27s+%27Gotta+
Brand+New+Bag%27.-a018065885 (accessed July 2014).

United Kingdom Tea Council. "The History of the Tea Bag." http://
www.tea.co.uk/thehistory-of-the-tea-bag (accessed July 2014).

Wikipedia. "Tea Bag." http://en.wikipedia.org/wiki/Tea_bag
(accessed July 2014).

Wikipedia. "History of Tea." http://en.wikipedia.org/wiki/History_
of_tea (accessed July 2014).

About Teatulia Organic Teas

Teatulia Organic Teas are sourced directly from their *own* garden in Northern Bangladesh and other like-minded gardens, with no long-term warehouse storage and no waiting around to be blended by a third party. Their organic tea garden is cultivated using only the natural farming practices developed by Japanese farmer, Masanobu Fukuoka. No machinery, pesticides, or unnatural irrigation is used in the cultivation of the garden. The resulting teas are great tasting, better for the land, its people, and the environment.

Started in 2000 to give back to the local community, the Teatulia Gardens were established as an enterprise that would give the local people a living wage while protecting and strengthening the environment. The Teatulia cooperative, or the KS Foundation, was launched to give back and provide a bright future to the Bangladeshi community. The cooperative has created innovative education, health, and cattle-lending programs for the people working in the garden and surrounding areas. All sales of Teatulia Organic Teas contribute to this mission, helping to better the lives of men, women, and children in the community while rebuilding the local ecosystem.

Teatulia has also created revolutionary green packaging. Their compostable, individually wrapped tea bags, frequently found in fine-dining restaurants and colleges and universities nationwide, are made from eco-friendly aspen and eucalyptus leaves, while Teatulia's signature eco-canisters are made from post-consumer waste and are 100 percent recyclable. All inks used in the packaging are soy-based, while the adhesives are water-based. And the tea bags are made of compostable corn silk or unbleached paper.

This all adds up to exquisite, clean, and smooth-tasting teas that support education, business, and health initiatives as well as demonstrate a thorough commitment to sustainability.

Index

102

104

Fahrenheit	Celcius	Gas Mark
225°	110°	¼
250°	120°	½
275°	140°	1
300°	150°	2
325°	160°	3
350°	180°	4
375°	190°	5
400°	200°	6
425°	220°	7
450°	230°	8

Ingredient	Cups/Tablespoons/ Teaspoons	Ounces	Grams/Milliliters
Fruits or veggies, chopped	1 cup	5 to 7 ounces	145 to 200 grams
Fruits or veggies, puréed	1 cup	8.5 ounces	245 grams
Honey or maple syrup	1 tablespoon	0.75 ounces	20 grams
Liquids: cream, milk, water, tea, spirits, or juice	1 cup	8 fluid ounces	240 milliliters
Salt	1 teaspoon	0.2 ounces	6 grams
Spices: cinnamon, cloves, ginger, or nutmeg (ground)	1 teaspoon	0.2 ounces	5 milliliters
Sugar, brown, firmly packed	1 cup	7 ounces	200 grams
Sugar, white	1 cup/1 tablespoon	7 ounces/0.5 ounces	200 grams/12.5 grams
Vanilla extract	1 teaspoon	0.2 ounces	4 grams

My Signature Tea Cocktail Recipes

_____
_____
_____
_____
_____
_____
_____
_____
_____
_____
_____
_____
_____
_____
_____
_____
_____
_____
_____
_____
_____

My Signature Tea Cocktail Recipes

Teatulia
ORGANIC TEAS

_____
_____
_____
_____
_____
_____
_____
_____
_____
_____
_____
_____
_____
_____
_____
_____
_____
_____
_____
_____

My Signature Tea Cocktail Recipes

_____

_____

_____

_____

_____

_____

_____

_____

_____

_____

_____

_____

_____

_____

_____

_____

_____

_____

_____

_____